H.P. Lovecraft
in Popular Culture

ALSO BY DON G. SMITH
AND FROM MCFARLAND

———————————

Lon Chaney, Jr.:
Horror Film Star, 1906–1973 (2004)

The Poe Cinema: A Critical Filmography
of Theatrical Releases Based on the Works
of Edgar Allan Poe (2003)

H.G. Wells on Film:
The Utopian Nightmare (2002)

H.P. Lovecraft in Popular Culture

The Works and Their Adaptations in Film, Television, Comics, Music and Games

Don G. Smith

McFarland & Company, Inc., Publishers
Jefferson, North Carolina, and London

LIBRARY OF CONGRESS CATALOGUING-IN-PUBLICATION DATA

Smith, Don G., 1950–
    H.P. Lovecraft in popular culture : the works and their
adaptations in film, television, comics, music and games /
Don G. Smith.
        p.   cm.
    Includes bibliographical references and index.

    ISBN 0-7864-2091-X (softcover : 50# alkaline paper)

    1. Lovecraft, H.P. (Howard Phillips), 1890–1937 — Adaptations —
History and criticism.   2. Lovecraft, H.P. (Howard Phillips), 1890–
1937 — Film and video adaptations.   3. Lovecraft, H.P. (Howard
Phillips), 1890–1937 — Appreciation.   4. Lovecraft, H.P. (Howard
Phillips), 1890–1937 — Influence.   5. Horror tales, American —
History and criticism.   6. Popular culture — History — 20th century.
7. Horror films — History and criticism.   8. Cthulhu (Fictitious
character)   9. Horror in mass media.   I. Title.
PS3523.O833Z865 2006
813'.52 — dc22   2005020847

British Library cataloguing data are available

Cover photograph ©2005 PhotoSpin

Manufactured in the United States of America

*McFarland & Company, Inc., Publishers
    Box 611, Jefferson, North Carolina 28640
    www.mcfarlandpub.com*

For Sandy Smith
and
for Joyce Carol Oates

Contents

Preface

Howard Phillips Lovecraft entered our world as an only child on August 20, 1890, in Providence, Rhode Island. His syphilitic father, a traveling salesman, suffered a seizure when the boy was only three and died in an insane asylum five years later. His overprotective mother shared child-rearing responsibilities with his two aunts and a grandfather, wealthy industrialist Whipple Phillips. Despite these early difficulties, Lovecraft began to read at the age of two, commenced writing his own stories and poems at seven, and learned Latin and Greek at eight. As a teenager he began producing his own journals on the subjects of chemistry and astronomy.

When Whipple Phillips died in 1904, Lovecraft and his mother were forced to move into a smaller house. Ill health plagued the boy, and in 1908 he suffered a nervous breakdown. Leaving Hope High School without graduating and being reclusively confined to his home for the next three years, he educated himself in philosophy, literature, and natural science.

In 1914, Lovecraft joined in the literary and political endeavors of both the United and National amateur press associations, producing 13 issues of his own journal, *The Conservative* (1915–1923). In 1918 his mother was confined to the same mental institution that had housed his father. Due to the nature of his early upbringing, Lovecraft fancied himself a gentleman, and though he lived in near poverty, was reluctant to write professionally. Urged by friends to publish his work,

1

he relented and from 1924 to 1938 placed most of his horror fiction and eerie poetry in *Weird Tales* magazine. In 1924, the same year he published "The Rats in the Walls," he was apparently asked to edit the publication. True to form, he refused. His greatest influences in those early years were Lord Dunsany and Edgar Allan Poe. Under inspiration from Lord Dunsany he wrote such dream stories as "The White Ship" (1919) and *The Dream-Quest of Unknown Kadath* (1926–27). In the tradition of Poe he wrote such tales as "The Outsider" (1921).

Lovecraft's mother died in 1921. Two months later he met, and three years later married, Sonia Haft Greene, a Ukrainian Jew several years older than he. The couple moved into Sonia's Brooklyn apartment, but when her hat shop business failed along with her health, she was forced to take a job in the Midwest. Left alone in Brooklyn, a city he disliked because of its noise and its foreigners, Lovecraft wrote few stories before effectively ending the marriage and returning to Providence. During that time, however, he did publish his now-famous "Supernatural Horror in Literature" in *Recluse*, an amateur publication. In that work, he demonstrated perceptive knowledge of the horror genre to which he was contributing.

Having returned to Providence in 1926, Lovecraft produced what are now regarded as his greatest works: "The Call of Cthulhu" (1926), *The Case of Charles Dexter Ward* (1927), "The Colour out of Space" (1927), "The Dunwich Horror" (1929) "The Whisperer in Darkness" (1930), "The Shadow over Innsmouth" (1931), *At the Mountains of Madness* (1931), and "The Shadow out of Time" (1934–35). Lovecraft's stories linked gothic themes and atmosphere to the science fiction genre in ways unique to the time. Though a mechanistic materialist and atheist, he described his writings as "cosmic." And indeed they were. Though often set in the author's transformed New England, the stories abound in pseudomythological gods from beyond the stars and in occult books such as the dreaded *Necronomicon* by the mad Arab Abdul Alhazred. Although Lovecraft never used the term, some of his stories are now considered to compose the "Cthulhu Mythos," which inspired additions by such weird fiction notables as August Derleth, Robert E. Howard, Robert Bloch, Clark Ashton Smith, Frank Belknap Long, Ramsey Campbell, and a host of others.

At the time of his death on March 15, 1937, Lovecraft had published only one book: *The Shadow over Innsmouth: And Other Stories of Horror* (1936). True to form, it was issued as a limited edition by a small press. Recognizing the value of what Lovecraft had done, August Derleth and Donald Wandrei founded Arkham House, a firm devoted to publishing Lovecraft's works in hardback. Their first venture, *The Outsider and Others* (1939), is a landmark in the history of weird fiction. Since then, Lovecraft's works have been consistently in print in both hardback and paperback editions. His five-volume *Selected Letters* was published between 1965 and 1976, and Lovecraft scholar S.T. Joshi republished his works in a corrected text between 1984 and 1989. Lovecraft's *Miscellaneous Writings* was published in 1995.

Testaments to Lovecraft's influence abound:

> Howard Phillips Lovecraft was the Copernicus of the horror story. He shifted the focus of supernatural dread from man and his little world and his gods, to the stars and the black and unplumbed gulfs of intergalactic space. To do this effectively, he created a new kind of horror story and new methods for telling it.
>
> — Fritz Leiber, Jr., author

> [Lovecraft] vehemently stood, in his letters, against the ravages of industrial civilization, which was attacking man at his deepest level: isolating him from the past, from the traditions of his race, tearing him from his native soil; in a word, alienating him.... In a society that is becoming each day more anesthetized and repressive, the fantastic is at once an evasion and the mobilization of anguish. It restores man's sense of the sacred or the sacrilegious; it above all gives back to him his lost depth. For the myth of the automobile, the washing machine, and the vacuum cleaner, for the modern myths of the new world that are merely surface myths, Lovecraft substituted the Cthulhu Mythos.
>
> — Maurice Levy, a leading
> Lovecraft scholar

> While outside the genre he may be a pygmy beside such classical giants as Poe, Hawthorne, and Melville, Lovecraft in the darkness of his vision can be compared as their spiritual heir.... As for twentieth century writers, he belongs in a broad

sense, as Darrell Schweitzer has suggested, "on a level with Borges and Franz Kafka."
                          — Peter Cannon, a leading Lovecraft scholar

Lovecraft is one of the few authors of whom I can honestly say that I have enjoyed every word of his stories.
                          — T.O. Mabbott, a leading Poe scholar

Poe and Lovecraft are our two American geniuses of fantasy, comparable each to the other, but incomparably superior to all the rest who follow in their wake.
                          — Robert Bloch, author

I discovered Lovecraft at age thirteen, and was never the same thereafter.
                          — F. Paul Wilson, author

H.P. Lovecraft is one of the absolute masters of the tale of supernatural dread and visionary horror, and among the writers whose work has been most crucial to the development of the field.... On a personal note, if I had not had his work on which to model my first serious efforts while learning my craft, I might well never have been heard of as a writer.
                          — Ramsey Campbell, author

As critic Barton L. St. Armand explains, Lovecraft is to the twentieth century what the gothic novelists and Romantic poets were to the eighteenth. In a world that sensitive souls viewed as stripped of wonder by natural science and industrialism, gothic novelists such as Horace Walpole, Gregory Lewis, and Mary Shelley offered antirationalistic visions of life, and poets such as William Wordsworth and Percy Shelley strove to restore wonder to our natural world. Lovecraft stands in a similar position in the twentieth century. Perhaps the Old Ones or Old Gods are waiting unseen for the chance to reclaim their dominion over both the world and humanity. Most gothic writers of the eighteenth century did not believe in ghosts, and Lovecraft did not believe in gods, strange or otherwise. Nevertheless, the point is the same. Humanity is dangerously alienated from the world. To the extent that he follows that theme, at least, Lovecraft is a modern author deserving our attention.

In this vein, S. T. Joshi stresses Lovecraft's anxiety over the decline of the West as expressed particularly in the prose poem "Nyarlathotep." Lovecraft partially linked this decline to the influx of foreigners in the early twentieth century. He was an anti–Semitic xenophobe and racist.

Lovecraft's influence has stretched far beyond the literary horror genre. A number of his works have been adapted as feature films, some have been adapted as television episodes, and many have been adapted as comic book tales. H.P. Lovecraft was even the name of a short-lived but influential rock band in the late 1960s, and his works have been adapted as video games. In addition, many artifacts of popular culture have been inspired by Lovecraft without credit. For a man who never aspired to recognition, his impact on popular culture has been considerable, and that is the focus of this book.

I first discovered Lovecraft as a ten-year-old in 1960 when my aunt bought me the Modern Library Giant *Great Tales of Terror and the Supernatural*, wherein appeared the author's "Rats in the Walls" and "Dunwich Horror." I learned years later that director John Carpenter was introduced to Lovecraft via the same book. As years passed, I encountered Lovecraft stories in any number of terror anthologies. I read nearly all of his work when a flood of paperback editions appeared in the early 1970s. Since then, I have tried on an amateur level to keep pace with Lovecraft scholarship and related matters.

In 2000, I published *The Poe Cinema*, which covered the films based on works by Edgar Allan Poe. In that book, I devoted considerable space to Lovecraft in the chapter on Poe's *Haunted Palace*, which was actually an adaptation of Lovecraft's *Case of Charles Dexter Ward*. After finishing *The Poe Cinema* I decided to write a general introduction exploring Lovecraft's influence on popular culture in general. There are other books that focus on a particular aspect of Lovecraft in popular culture, but this is the only book to serve as a general introduction. As such, this is in no way a definitive volume, as I intended my *Poe Cinema* to be. In writing it, I pay a debt to one who, like Poe, influenced my life and became a part of me.

PART ONE

The Writings of H.P. Lovecraft

H.P. Lovecraft was a creature of the pulps. Such magazines were printed on cheap paper, featured lurid covers and provocatively titled stories, and sold for between five cents and a quarter. Largely aimed at American males, the stories provided adventure (e.g. *Spicy Adventure Stories, Rip-Roaring Western*), mystery (e.g. *Spicy Detective Stories, Thrilling Detective, Thrilling Mystery,* and *Black Mask*), sex (e.g. *Sizzling Romances, Stolen Sweets,* and *Saucy Movie Tales*), horror (e.g. *Ghost Stories, Strange Stories,* and *Horror Stories*), and science fiction (e.g. *Thrilling Wonder Stories, Fantastic Story, Amazing Stories,* and *Planet Stories*). As one might expect, the pulps published much ephemeral trash. On the other hand, they also published some of the most important writers and popular artists of the twentieth century.

Lovecraft's major publisher of choice was *Weird Tales*, founded in 1922 by Clark Henneberger. With Edwin Baird as editor, the magazine stuggled along until 1924 when May/July issue featured "The Loved One," written by C.M. Eddy, Jr. (and revised by Lovecraft). The graphic tale of necrophilia caused a firestorm in the industry and garnered considerable public notoriety. Henneberger tried to bring Lovecraft on board as editor, but the author refused, after which Farnsworth Wright landed the job. Although the magazine continued to struggle, it published some of the century's finest names in horror and science fiction: Robert Bloch, Ray Bradbury, Robert E. Howard, Seabury Quinn, August Derleth, Clark Ashton Smith, and, of course, H.P. Lovecraft. The "Unique Magazine" also reprinted tales by such luminaries as Edgar A. Poe, Sir Arthur Conan Doyle, Algernon Black-wood, E.F. Benson, Gaston Leroux, Robert Louis Stevenson, and H.G. Wells.

What money Lovecraft made, he made from selling stories to the pulps, along with doing some ghostwriting for ridiculously low fees. In this, Lovecraft is quite different from earlier horror and science fiction writers (such as Poe and Hawthorne) who wrote for mainstream publications and then collected their works in books.

The following is an annotated bibliography of Lovecraft's horror and science fiction tales. Each title is followed by the date Lovecraft wrote the story and then (if known) by the name of the magazine in which the story appeared. A short summary usually follows the story, sometimes with a note of the literary sources that probably inspired it.

Also included are stories written by Lovecraft in collaboration with other writers. In these cases, the title is followed by the date when Lovecraft collaborated, and then by the name of the collaborator. For these, no plot summaries are provided.

"The Beast in the Cave" (1905)

The narrator, on a guided tour of a cave once occupied by a col-ony of consumptives, wanders off alone and becomes lost in complete darkness. Having given up hope of rescue, he becomes frightened when a four-footed beast approaches in the darkness. The narrator fires rocks in the direction of the beast and mortally wounds it. The tour guide arrives, and they discover that the white ape-like creature lying before them had at one time been a man.

"The Alchemist" (1908)

Antoine, the narrator, is the last of a long line of noblemen cursed by Charles Le Sorcier six centuries before. All died at the age of 32, and now the narrator faces the same fate. Antoine, after mortally wounding a stranger in an abandoned part of the chateau, is aston-ished to discover that the stranger is Charles Le Sorcier, the alchemist who discovered the secret of eternal life and exacted his revenge over the centuries.

"The Tomb" (1917). *The Vagrant*, March 1922.

The narrator, Jervas Dudley, becomes haunted by spirits when, as a boy, he sleeps near an ancient tomb occupied by the wicked Hyde family. Over the years he returns frequently to the tomb, believing that he will eventually be buried in an empty coffin resting in the vault.

"Dagon" (1917)

During World War I, the narrator escapes from a torpedoed vessel and arrives in a part of the Pacific where there have been recent disturbances at the bottom of the sea. On a slimy land mass coughed up from the depths, he discovers a large monolith depicting humanoid creatures worshipping Dagon, the fish-god of the Philistines. Then the fish-god appears!

"Polaris" (May? 1918). *The Philosopher*, December 1920.

While his thoughts are fixed on the polestar, the narrator learns of the lost polar land of Lomar where people are under attack by invading Eskimos. Is he experiencing a memory from a past life? Is Lomar a real place with real people in danger? The narrator does not know, but ever after he can sleep only on cloudy nights.

"Beyond the Wall of Sleep" (1919). *Pine Cones*, October 1919.

When Slater, a drunken backwoodsman, commits murder and is incarcerated in an asylum, he tells of an alternate reality occupied by a race of luminous beings to which he feels he belongs. The narrator, an asylum employee, suspects a grain of truth in the story and decides to explore Slater's mind via an electrical device that joins their two intellects. When the experiment begins, a voice informs the narrator that Slater's dead body is possessed by a wandering, luminous intelligence. It appears that a battle is raging over time and space, a truth borne out by an ordinary astronomical discovery.

"Memory" (1919)

A prose poem. In the valley of Nis, the Genie of the moonbeams asks the Daemon of the valley who built the ruins that lie in the valley. The Daemon identifies herself as Memory and attributes the ruins to an extinct species called Man. Possible source: "The Conversation of Eiros and Charmion" by E.A. Poe.

"Old Bugs" (1919)

No information seems to be available about this story.

"The Transition of Juan Romero" (September 16, 1919)

In the mining country of the American West, the narrator and his new friend, Mexican laborer Juan Romero, are present when dynamite opens a new vein. Along with gold, however, they discover a mysterious deep gorge. That night the narrator is awakened by Oriental chants that he heard while in India and by a throbbing deep in the ground. Romero hears these sounds as well and dashes into the dark cavern, followed by the narrator. In the depths of the earth, Romero falls victim to strange indescribable beings that effect his "transition." The narrator flees in terror. In the morning, he awakens in his bunk to find a group of men examining the corpse of Juan Romero, who must have died during the night due to a lighting bolt that hit the camp, closing the mine. The narrator has no explanation for the strange events, but what may have been just a dream continues over the years to disturb his peace.

"The White Ship" (November 1919). *The United Amateur*, November 1919.

The narrator, lighthouse keeper Basil Elton, has long pondered the ocean's secrets. One night, a mysterious white ship emerges from the fog and carries Elton to a number of allegorical ports such as the City of a Thousand Wonders and the Land of Pleasures Unattainable. He lingers long in Sona-Nyl, the Land of Fancy, where life is a pleasant dream. Curiosity eventually drives him to sail on in search of the Land of Hope. Possible sources: "Wonderful Window" and "The Dream of King Karna-Vootra" by Lord Dunsany, and the *Republic* by Plato.

"The Doom That Came to Sarnath" (December 3, 1919). *Scot*, June 1920.

In the land of Mnar a species of reptile people worship Bokrug, "the great water-lizard," in the city of Ib. Men arrive in Mnar and establish the city of Sarnath. As time passes, the men grow to hate the lizard people, destroy them, throw their bodies into a lake, and carry the green idol of Bokrug back to Sarnath. The night of their arrival, however, the priest dies, the idol disappears, and strange lights emanate from the burial lake. Over the next millennium Sarnath prospers, but on the thousandth anniversary of the genocide, lights reappear in the lake and the lizard people emerge to doom Sarnath. Possible source: the writings of Lord Dunsany.

"The Statement of Randolph Carter" (December 1919). *The Vagrant*, May 1920.

Authorities question Randolph Carter about the disappearance of his friend Harley Warren. According to Carter, the two set out to explore an ancient tomb wherein Warren expected to find something fantastic. Warren decided to descend the stone steps into the tomb alone while staying in contact with Carter via a telephone-like device. Warren never returned from the tomb, but through the phone wire, something unholy addressed Carter from the depths of the tomb.

"The Terrible Old Man" (January 28, 1920). *The Tryout*, July 1921.

In the strange village of Kingsport, Massachusetts, an old ex-seafarer inhabits a shunned house wherein he keeps bottles with lead pendulums inside. He addresses the bottles by name, and they seem to answer. Three ruffians enter the house and try to rob the old man, but they pay for their mistake with their lives. Possible sources: "The Probable Adventure of the Three Literary Men," "How Nuth Would Have Practiced His Art upon the Gnoles," and *A Night at the Inn* by Lord Dunsany.

"The Tree" (1920). *The Tryout*, October 1921.

Two sculptors, Kalos and Musides, are close friends until the tyrant of Syracuse asks them to compete in making a statue of him. Musides poisons Kalos, but Kalos gets revenge when a tree grows out of his tomb and discharges a limb upon Musides' house. Possible source: Greek and Roman mythology and works of Nathaniel Hawthorne.

"The Cats of Ulthar" (June 15, 1920). *The Tryout*, November 1920.

According to the law of Ulthar, no one may kill a cat. Before the law was passed, an old couple killed every cat they could get their hands on. One day a caravan passes through, including an orphan boy named Menes, who soon finds his black kitten missing. Hearing of the cruel exploits of the old couple, Menes performs a rite of conjuration, and that night all the cats of Ulthar disappear. The cats return the next morning, well fed, but all that remains of the old couple is a pair of skeletons. Possible source: the works of Lord Dunsany.

"The Temple" (1920). *Weird Tales*, September 1925.

During World War I, a German U-29 sinks a British ship and picks up the corpse of one of the victims. In the corpse's possession is a strange ivory carving of a youth's head. As days pass, members of the German crew go mad and commit suicide or are shot by the captain. The U-29 encounters mechanical difficulties that render it a drifting derelict. The only two left aboard are the captain and the first officer. When the first officer goes mad and commits suicide, the captain is left alone with the carved head to await death. The ship settles to the bottom of the sea amid the ruins of lost Atlantis. The captain decides to spend his final hours exploring Atlantis in a diving suit.

"Facts Concerning the Late Arthur Jermyn and His Family" (1920). Appeared as "The White Ape" in *Weird Tales*, April 1924.

Beginning in the eighteenth century, the family of African explorer Arthur Jermyn is afflicted with hereditary madness and physical deformities. Sir Wade had returned from the Congo with tales of a dying city occupied by a vanishing race presided over by a white ape goddess. He had also returned with a wife. The two made subsequent trips back to the dying city until, on the last trip, Sir Wade's wife failed to return with him. Sir Wade was then confined to an insane asylum. Arthur Jermyn, Sir Wade's great-great-great-grandson, decides to investigate his family's history and acquires the mummy of the ape woman who was Sir Wade's wife.

"The Street" (1920?). *The Wolverine*, September 1920.

This prose poem tells the story of a street in a small New England town from its origin as the perimeter of a Puritan fortress till its destruction in an anarchist uprising.

"Poetry and the Gods" (1920) with Anna Helen Crofts

"Celephais" (early November 1920). *The Rainbow*, May 1922.

Fed up with the ugliness of modern London, the narrator imagines a world called Celephais which he, taking the name Kuranes, visits in his dreams. After several visits to Celephais, during which time he becomes a hero to the dream world's population, he finds he can no longer find his way there in his dreams. He then resorts to hashish to conjure the visions necessary for his return. Finally, a group of knights arrive and escort Kuranes to Celephais, where he is crowned king and pronounced god and creator.

"From Beyond" (November 16, 1920). *The Fantasy Fan*, June 1934.

Crawford Tillinghast invites the narrator to witness a demonstration of a newly created machine that will allow people to remain in our three-dimensional world while being able to see into another dimension. Tillinghast's servants have disappeared and the mad scientist apparently has the same in mind for his friend, the narrator. When a creature from another dimension attacks, the narrator fires a gun at the machine, ending the experiment and causing Tillinghast's death by apoplexy.

"Nyarlathotep" (early December 1920)

A prose poem. In it the narrator reports that Nyarlathotep comes out of Egypt, having risen from the darkness of 27 centuries. Political and social upheaval erupt, threatening the survival of civilization.

"The Picture in the House" (December 12, 1920). *The National Amateur*, July 1919.

Having taken refuge from a storm in one of the Arkham region's seemingly deserted farmhouses, the narrator encounters an old man who asks him to translate from a book about the Congo. A picture in the book depicting "a butcher's shop of the cannibal Antiques" gives the narrator pause. The old man denies that he has ever engaged in the act of cannibalism, after which a drop of red liquid falls from the ceiling. The narrator narrowly escapes when lightning destroys the house.

"The Crawling Chaos" (1920–21) with Winifred V. Jackson

"Ex Oblivione" (1920–21). *United Amateur*, 1921.

This philosophical short piece proposes that life is only an interruption of a better state of being.

"The Nameless City" (January 1921). *Transatlantic Circular*, undated.

An explorer narrates the story of his discovery of a city that was already in ruins in the ancient days of Chaldea. He finds temples there with ceilings too low to accommodate human beings and follows a passageway leading deep into the earth to a display of reptilian creatures' remains. The narrator then arrives at a glowing brass door. He opens the door and sees a sight so terrible that he flees the city and leaves its location a secret. In this story Lovecraft first mentions the mad Arab poet Abdul Alhazred, author of the dreaded *Necronomicon*.

"The Quest of Iranon" (February 28, 1921). *The Galleon*, July–August 1935.

A balladeer and dreamer named Iranon travels the world searching for his native city of Aira, where songs and dreams are valued most highly. In the city of granite, which is devoted to labor, Iranon meets a boy named Romnod, and the two travel together. In the city of Oonai, a place of song and debauchery, Romnod dies, and Iranon goes on alone. Years later, an aging Iranon learns from an old shepherd who knew him as a youth that the city of Aira was only a fantasy. Iranon then commits suicide by walking into quicksand. Possible source: the writings of Lord Dunsany.

"The Moon-Bog" (March 1921). *Weird Tales*, June 1926.

Denys Barry travels to the castle of his ancestors in his native Ireland and decides to drain the bog near the castle. Barry wants to farm the land under the bog, but he also wants to investigate the legend of an ancient Greek city rumored to exist there. When work begins on the bog, Barry's laborers begin to act strangely, and lights and sounds emanate from the site where the ancient city is supposed to be. Then, on one moonlit night, Barry spots a grotesque form on the tower of the moon-bog's ruin.

"The Outsider" (1921). *Weird Tales*, April 1926.

The narrator has dwelt in isolation in the old castle for as long as he can remember. Fearing that the forests around the castle will not allow his escape, he decides to scale a soaring black tower that seems to reach into the clouds. When he reaches the top, he forces open a door and finds himself on ground level. Exploring his new environment, he enters a castle where a party is being held. When he enters the presence of the revelers, they scream in fear. Sudenly he encounters a detestable, eaten-away travesty of the human form. Sickened by the sight, the narrator returns to his desolate home underground, realizing that the putrid corpse he saw was his own reflection in polished glass. Possible source: the writings of E.A. Poe.

"The Other Gods" (August 14, 1921). *The Fantasy Fan*, November 1933.

Barzai the Wise of Ulthar knows the legend of the peak of Hatheg-Kla, where the gods of the earth once played before being invaded by humanity. With a priest named Atal, the ambitious and vain Barzai mounts an expedition to the mountain in order to see the gods, whom he believes still return there sometimes to play. They find the gods but discover that these gods are protected by even higher gods. Atal returns alone and cannot thereafter be persuaded to pray for Barzai's soul. Possible source: the writings of Lord Dunsany.

"The Music of Erich Zann" (December 1921). *The National Amateur*, March 1922.

The setting is Paris. Erich Zann is a mute old genius who makes a living playing violin in a theater orchestra. Alone in his mysterious room, however, he composes music of his own that no one is allowed to hear — music that invites contact with beings from another cosmos.

"Herbert West — Reanimator" (September 1921 to mid–1922). *Home Brew*, serialized February–July 1922.

Herbert West, a medical student at Miskatonic University, and his aide engage in experiments to reanimate the dead. In Part One, "The Plague-Demon," West creates a monster from deceased plague victims. In Part Two, "Six Shots by Moonlight," West, recently graduated from medical school, continues his reanimation experiments with a victim of a fatal air crash. The result is a zombie. In Part Three, "The Scream of the Dead," West reanimates Robert Leavitt of Saint Louis. Instead of revealing to West the secrets of death, the resurrected corpse reveals his tragic last moments before dying. In Part Five, "The Horror from the Shadows," West, now practicing medicine in Boston, joins the army and finds himself a medic on Flanders battlefield during World War II. In an experiment with distasteful results, West reanimates the headless body of his friend, Major Eric Clapham-Lee. In Part Six, "The Tomb-Legions," West returns to Boston and is living in an old house built over an ancient burial ground. Again West raises the dead, and again the results are not to his liking.

"Hypnos" (May 1922). *The National Amateur*, May 1923.

The philosophically inclined narrator discovers an unconscious bearded stranger. The narrator and the revived stranger go to the former's house in Kent and embark on a series of mystical experiments involving narcotic drugs. As a result, the two age rapidly, and the stronger man begins having distressing nightmares about some unknown thing in the vicinity of the constellation of Corona Borealis.

"What the Moon Brings" (June 5, 1922). *The National Amateur*, 1923.

The narrator hates the moon because its rays reveal to him that a sea reef is really the forehead of a giant being.

"Azathoth" (June 1922)

"The Horror at Martin's Beach" (1922) with Sonia Davis

"Four o'Clock (1922) with Sonia Davis

"The Hound" (September 1922). *Weird Tales*, February 1925.

The narrator, two diabolists, and their friend St. John enjoy discussing the aesthetics of the macabre, which leads them to grave robbing. When they open the grave of a ghoul and remove the corpse's jade amulet, they unleash the vengeful monster of the title. Probable sources: *The Hound of the Baskervilles* by A. Conan Doyle, "The Damned Thing" by Ambrose Bierce, and "The Raven," "The Masque of the Red Death," and "The Oblong Box" by E.A. Poe.

"The Lurking Fear" (November 1922). *Home Brew*, serialized January–April 1923.

The narrator and two companions travel to the Martense mansion atop Tempest Mountain in the Catskills to investigate reported tragedies. It seems that during thunderstorms, something dwelling on Tempest Mountain murders squatters and local townspeople. The narrator discovers that the Martense family has degenerated into thousands of cannibals who dwell under the mounds and ridges surrounding the mansion.

"The Rats in the Walls" (August or September 1923). *Weird Tales*, March 1924.

The narrator, a modern descendent of the old English de la Poer family, returns from Boston to the family seat at Exham Priory. Upon arriving, he finds that the locals fear him and his family name, suggesting that some secret horror is associated with his heritage. He also learns that hordes of rats run through the walls of the priory. When his cat disappears, the narrator explores the levels below the priory and makes some hideous discoveries.

"The Ghost Eater" (1923) with C.M. Eddy, Jr.

"The Loved One (1923) with C.M. Eddy, Jr.

"The Festival" (1923). *Weird Tales*, January 1925.

The narrator accepts a request that he participate in ancient Yule rites to be held in the ancient colonial-period village of Kingsport, Massachusetts. The ritual, which the narrator's ancestors brought to New England in the 1600s, begins with a procession from a house in Green Lane to the church on Central Hill. The procession then descends into the catacombs below the church, where the participants encounter horror.

"Imprisoned with the Pharaohs" (February–March, 1924). *Weird Tales*, serialized May–July 1924. Published as by Harry Houdini.

This story, ghostwritten by Lovecraft for escape artist Harry Houdini, recounts Houdini's travels during which he is captured by Arab thugs, tied, and thown into a pit in the desert near the Sphinx. Before escaping, Houdini witnesses a hideous, ancient ritual.

"The Shunned House" (October 1924). *Weird Tales*, October 1937.

Dr. Whipple, an antiquarian, and his nephew, the narrator, investigate the strange Harris house in Providence, Rhode Island, where several generations of inhabitants had suffered under what appeared to be a curse. Dr. Whipple's research reveals that the house was built on a long abandoned graveyard of mysterious Huguenots. Inside the house, a humanoid mist rises from the dirt floor of the cellar and gobbles up Dr. Whipple. The next day, the narrator discovers a giant jelly-like monster dwelling under the house and destroys it with concentrated sulfuric acid. Possible source: *Myths and Legends of Our Lives* by Charles M. Skinner.

"The Horror at Red Hook" (August 1–2, 1925). *Weird Tales*, January 1927.

The setting is Brooklyn. Occultist Robert Suydam, who maintains a mansion in Flatbush, has befriended a bunch of foreign ruffians occupying tenements in the squalid Red Hook district. Police detective Thomas Malone seeks justice when Suydam and his bride are mutilated and murdered on their wedding night in Suydam's Cunard liner stateroom. Malone follows the clues to Red Hook and makes a terrifying discovery.

"He" (August 11, 1925). *Weird Tales*, September 1926.

While searching for antique architecture in Greenwich Village, the narrator encounters a mysterious stranger who offers a unique architectural tour. The stranger leads the narrator to a house built before the village ever existed and introduces himself as an eccentric magician dressed in eighteenth century clothing. Soon afterward, the stranger performs a conjuration, and the horror begins.

"In the Vault" (1925). *The Tryout*, November 1925.

An undertaker who routinely cuts corners in his business practices pays the price for such activities when trapped in the receiving room of the Peck Valley Cemetery.

"The Descendant" (1926?)

"Cool Air" (1926). *Tales of Magic and Mystery*, March 1928.

The narrator rents a room in a brownstone house in New York. There, he meets Dr. Munoz, a Spanish aristocrat who claims to have a disease requiring him to stay in temperatures below 60 degrees. As Munoz's condition worsens he increasingly lowers the temperature in his room via a refrigeration system. As temperatures rise in New York and the system malfunctions, the narrator makes a most unwelcome discovery.

"The Call of Cthulhu" (Summer 1926). *Weird Tales*, 1928.

The great sea god, Cthulhu, rules the underwater city of R'lyeh, dreaming until the day that it and its city can rise up and possess the earth. The narrator follows news reports from around the world and discovers the terrible fate that awaits humanity when Cthulhu rises. Possible source: the Norweigan myth of the Kraken and the poem "The Kraken" by Alfred, Lord Tennyson.

"Two Black Bottles" (July–October 1926), with Wilfred B. Talman.

"Pickman's Model" (1926). *Weird Tales*, October 1927.

Richard Pickman is not liked by his fellow artists because of the gruesome subjects he paints and because of the secrecy regarding his inspiration. Pickman, an owner of a copy of the dreaded *Necronomicon*, paints his bloodthirsty ghouls from life.

"The Silver Key" (1926). *Weird Tales*, January 1939.

In this dream story, Randolph Carter attempts to escape the everyday world with help from a silver key, inscribed with hieroglyphics, that unlocks a door sending him into an alternative reality. Possible source: Lord Dunsany's dream stories.

"The Strange High House in the Mist" (1926). *Weird Tales*, October 1931.

Philosopher Thomas Olney comes upon a cottage high on a cliff above Kingsport, Massachusetts. The house proves to be a halfway house between two dimensions of reality.

The Dream-Quest of Unknown Kadath (1926). *The Arkham Sampler*, serialized winter–autumn 1948.

Randoph Carter entered a dream world in this, one of Lovecraft's longest projects. Unfortunately, the project remained unfinished. Still, the final product does not suffer, because the whole work is a striking but plotless play of imagery. Possible source: Lord Dunsany's dream stories.

The Case of Charles Dexter Ward (1927–1928). *Weird Tales*, serialized May and July 1921.

Charles Dexter Ward, a student, investigates the history of his ancestor, Joseph Curwin. Ward soon falls under the spell of Curwin's plan to learn forbidden secrets from other dimensions of reality and use that knowledge, with that of other magicians, to expose earth to horrors from beyond.

"The Colour Out of Space" (1927). *Amazing Stories*, September 1927.

A meteorite crashes on the land of farmer Nahum Gardner. First the flora and fauna of the area are affected, then the farm animals, then Nahum and his family. By the time the area in question becomes a "blasted heath," madness and horror rule the little farm outside of Arkham.

"The Very Old Folk" (November 2, 1927)

"The Last Test" (1927) with Adolphe de Castro

"The Curse of Yig" (1928) with Zealia Bishop

"The Dunwich Horror" (summer 1928). *Weird Tales*, April 1929.

Goat-like Wilbur Whateley, latest in a family line of black magicians, attempts to steal the dreaded *Necronomicon* from the Miskatonic University Library. His goal is to perform forbidden ceremonies among the ancient stones of the Devil's Hopyard on Sentinel Hill. Dr. Henry Armitage tries to stop him but soon finds himself battling Wilbur's twin brother, a tentacled monster who takes after the boys' father, a creature from another dimension.

"The Electric Executioner" (1929?) with Adolphe de Castro

"The Mound" (December 1929 to early 1930) with Zealia Bishop

"Medusa's Coil" (May 1930) with Zealia Bishop

"The Whisperer in Darkness" (1930). *Weird Tales*, August 1931.

When floods in New Hampshire and Vermont rekindle strange folk legends, literature professor Albert Wilmarth decides to investigate. Do monsters really lurk in the hills? Wilmarth is skeptical, but a series of letters from area native Henry Akeley entices him to visit and learn for himself. And learn he does — of the fungus creatures of Yuggoth.

"At the Mountains of Madness" (1931). *Astounding Stories*, serialized February–April 1936.

Miskatonic University conducts an Antarctic expedition to find out what happened to an expedition that never returned. It seems that the first group disappeared after discovering a fossilized life form. Professor Danforth and a graduate student continue the investigation and discover the ruins of a city once occupied by the Old Ones, half-vegetable, half-animal, squidlike things with starfish heads. Through rock carvings, Danforth and the student learn of the Old Ones' journey from outer space to Earth and their subsequent history — which is not yet over. The novella was inspired by Poe's "The Narrative of A. Gordon Pym."

"The Shadow over Innsmouth" (1931). *Weird Tales*, January 1942.

People avoid the coastal town of Innsmouth, which has a bad reputation due to the shadowy Esoteric Cult of Dagon that thrives there. The narrator, who is on a sightseeing tour, becomes interested in Innsmouth and decides to go there for a day. When his bus breaks down, he is forced to spend the night. It is then that he learns the secret of Devil's Reef and discovers that the locals are evolving into fish creatures.

"The Trap" (1931) with Henry S. Whitehead

"The Dreams in the Witch House" (January to February 28, 1932). *Weird Tales*, July 1933.

Walter Gilman, a student at Miskatonic University, rents a garret room in a house formerly owned by a reputed witch. According to legend, the architectural design of the house allowed the witch to escape into another dimension. The witch and her familiar, a rat named Brown Jenkin, begin appearing in Gilman's dreams. Worse follows.

"The Man of Stone" (1932) with Hazel Heald

"The Horror in the Museum" (October 1932) with Hazel Heald

"Through the Gates of the Silver Key" (October 1932 to April 1933) with E. Hoffmann Price

"Winged Death" (1933) with Hazel Heald

"Out of the Eons" (1933) with Hazel Heald

"The Thing on the Doorstep" (August 21–24, 1933). *Weird Tales*, January 1937.

Edward Pickman Derby, a student of the occult, meets Asenath Waite, a descendant of the Waite family of Innsmouth and reputedly the daughter of a dangerous wizard. Edward and Asenath marry, and Asenath leads Edward further into occultism than he had ever dared to go. When Edward tries to break free of Asanath, horror follows.

"The Horror in the Burying Ground" (1933–1935) with Hazel Heald

"The Book" (late 1933?)

"The Tree on the Hill" (May 1934) with Duane W. Rimel

"The Battle That Ended the Century" (June 1934) with R.H. Barlow

"The Shadow Out of Time" (1934). *Astounding Stories*, June 1936.

Nathaniel Wingate Peaslee, an economist at Miskatonic University, lapses into a form of chronic amnesia for five years, during which he conducts studies of human culture as though he is learning of it for the first time. Upon recovery, he is haunted by memories of the dreams he had during his illness — dreams involving a city that existed 150 million years before humanity. Later he realizes that his mind and that of an alien from another world have exchanged bodies.

"Till A' the Seas" (January 1935) with R.H. Barlow

"Collapsing Cosmoses" (June 1935) with R.H. Barlow

"The Challenge from Beyond" (August 1935) with C.L. Moore, A. Merritt, Robert E. Howard, and Frank Belknap Long

"The Diary of Alonzo Typer" (October 1935) with Brian Lumley

"The Haunter of the Dark" (November 1935). *Weird Tales,* December 1936.

Horror story author Robert Blake moves to Providence, Rhode Island, from Wisconsin. He becomes interested in the Free-Will Baptist Church on Federal Hill, and soon discovers that it was once used by a cult that worshipped alien gods such as Yog-Sothoth, Azazoth, and Nyarlathotep. Blake finds that a bizarre creature inhabits the church steeple and can prowl forth at night.

Lovecraft wrote this story in answer to Robert Bloch's "The Shambler from the Stars," a Cthulhu Mythos tale in which a character based on Lovecraft is horribly murdered by occult forces. Both stories were all in good fun (if you were in on the joke).

"In the Walls of Eryx" (January 1936) with Kenneth Sterling

"The Night Ocean" (autumn 1936?) with R.H. Barlow

"The Disinterment" (1936?) with Duane W. Rimel

PART TWO

The Cthulhu Mythos

As noted in the preface, many of Lovecraft's stories are considered to compose what critics call the "Cthulhu Mythos." The best relatively short explanation of this literary phenomenon is provided by Chris Jarocha-Ernst in introducing his "Bibliography of the Cthulhu Mythos":

> The Cthulhu Mythos is a name given to the collected fiction, both prose and poetry, about a set of alien beings, invented by H.P. Lovecraft, his friends, and his admirers. It is what is today termed a "shared world": a number of writers use the same settings, characters, objects, and concepts in otherwise unrelated stories (i.e., it's not necessarily a series, though some series have been set in the Mythos). Most often, these are horror stories, though the Mythos does include science fiction, high fantasy, sword-and-sorcery, and, in at least one case, mainstream fiction.
>
> In the world of the Cthulhu Mythos, alien beings known to us only as the Great Old Ones came to this planet eons ago and ruled. Through unknowable events (some claim a cosmic war with opposing entities, some merely a time of rest), these beings lost their hold and are now either asleep, somehow restricted to certain areas, or located elsewhere in time and space. Here on Earth, primal memories of these beings gave birth to many of humanity's diverse mythologies, and the Great Old Ones were revered as gods. As always, there were those who would exchange their very souls for a taste of terrestrial

power, and who dared to record their rites in blasphemous
books, and so the worship of the Great Old Ones began and
continues in secrecy to this day. Occasionally, an innocent
learns the horrendous truths behind the sheer veil of reality
and glimpses the ultratelluric chasms that exist, unknown to
most, beneath our mundane existence. The Cthulhu Mythos
stories chronicle the adventures of such unfortunates, frequently
in as high-blown a style as the later sentences of this paragraph
are in.*

Lovecraft's Cthulhu Mythos stories obviously reflect the author's
own materialistic worldview that human beings occupy no special place
in the universe. At times, those who worship beings from another world
or dimension side against humanity, and the outcome is unclear. This
distrust of "the other" runs through Lovecraft's fiction and reflects his
own perspective on immigration and the destruction of Western civilization.

It would be difficult, even if possible, to read every Cthulhu
Mythos story ever written. Chris Jarocha-Ernst's "Bibliography of the
Cthulhu Mythos" lists about 1,000 stories. The focus of this book is
on H.P. Lovecraft in popular culture, and only peripherally on other
writers who were influenced by Lovecraft. Those interested in the
broader Cthulhu Mythos perspective may find Jarocha-Ernst's website
a good starting point.

In *Lovecraft: A Look Behind the Cthulhu Mythos* (1972), Lin Carter
provides a "complete bibliography" up to the publication date. That
bibliography is included here with the addition of the place and date
the stories were published, followed by a brief synopsis. Comments
are added only for the pieces the author has read. Annotations of
Lovecraft's own stories appeared in Part One, and so are not repeated
here. Comments are added, however, on a few other Mythos writings by Lovecraft that are not stories. Happy hunting, you Mythos
maniacs!

*Jarocha-Ernst, Chris. *Klarkash-Ton and the Cthulhu Mythos*. 1996. The Eldritch Dark.
2005 <www.eldritchdark.com/bio/cas_and_the_cthulhu_mythos.html.

By H.P. Lovecraft

1. "The Nameless City." *Weird Tales*, November 1921.

2. "The Hound." *Weird Tales*, February 1924.

3. "The Festival." *Weird Tales*, January 1925.

4. "The Call of Cthulhu." *Weird Tales*, February 1928.

5. "The Dunwich Horror." *Weird Tales*, April 1929.

6. "The Whisperer in Darkness." *Weird Tales*, August 1931.

7. *The Shadow over Innsmouth*. Pa.: Visionary Press, 1936.

8. "At the Mountains of Madness." Three-part serial. *Astounding Stories*, February, March, and April 1936.

9. "The Dreams in the Witch House." *Weird Tales*, July 1933.

10. "The Thing on the Doorstep." *Weird Tales*, January 1937.

11. "The Shadow out of Time." *Astounding Stories*, June 1936.

12. "The Haunter of the Dark." *Weird Tales*, December 1936.

13. *History and Chronology of the "Necronomicon."* Ala.: The Rebel Press, 1936.

    This is Lovecraft's tongue-in-cheek "historical account" of his fictional *Necronomicon*. Over the years, many people have searched bookstores and antiquarian dealers for copies of this dreaded, nonexistent book.

14. *Fungi from Yuggoth*. Brochure. Cal.: F.A.P.A., 1941.

    This is a long poem by Lovecraft.

By H.P. Lovecraft, A. Merritt, C.L. Moore, Robert E. Howard and Frank Belknap Long

1. "The Challenge from Beyond." *Fantasy Magazine*, September 1935.

    Lovecraft and his writing circle produced this story in round-robin format, Lovecraft's contribution being the longest and best. In the story, a mysterious cube draws a man's mind to another planet where the man enters another body and eventually becomes a god.

By H.P. Lovecraft and August Derleth

After Lovecraft's death, Derleth lifted some passages and ideas from Lovecraft's notes, wrote tales around them, and published the following stories as "collaborations" with H.P. Lovecraft. Though Lovecraft was the obvious inspiration, the stories themselves are almost wholly written by Derleth.

1. *The Lurker on the Threshold.* Wisc.: Arkham House, 1945.

Derleth was able to "collaborate" with Lovecraft by writing a novel in Lovecraftian style around two brief and apparently disconnected passages from Lovecraft's notes. The story, set near Arkham, Mass., concerns a man who inherits an ancient ancestral estate and discovers that the ancestor was a wizard. Yog Sothoth makes an appearance.

2. "The Survivor." *Weird Tales*, July 1954.

The narrator rents the old Charriere house in Providence and discovers that the previous owner was a scientist experimenting with reptile cells and immortality. The story has echoes in "The Shuttered Room," another Lovecraft-Derleth "collaboration."

3. "The Gable Window." *Saturn*, May 1957.

The narrator moves into his cousin Wilbur's house and discovers that his relative had been a wizard prone to conjure creatures from another dimension through a gable window. The narrator repeats the process and finds himself attacked by those very creatures, who can see him as well as he can see them. The story is reminiscent of Lovecraft's "From Beyond."

4. "The Lamp of Alhazred." *The Magazine of Fantasy and Science Fiction*, October 1957.

Ward Phillips gains possession of a lamp once owned by the author of *The Necronomicon*. Derleth lifted passages from Lovecraft's letters to justify the "collaboration."

5. "The Shadow out of Space," in *The Shuttered Room and Other Pieces*. Wisc.: Arkham House, 1959.

Members of the Great Race transfer Piper's mind into a body of one of their own, and a Great One inhabits Piper's earthly frame.

6. "The Shuttered Room," in *The Shuttered Room and Other Pieces*. Wisc.: Arkham House, 1959.

Abner Whateley goes to Dunwich after word of his grandfather's death. Upon arrival, he receives written information from his deceased relative to destroy the mill part of the house and kill any living thing he finds there. Abner doesn't destroy the mill end of the house and lives to regret it. This story is an attempted synthesis of the Dunwich and Innsmouth legends.

7. "The Fisherman of Falcon Point," in *The Shuttered Room and Other Pieces*. Wisc.: Arkham House, 1959.

Fisherman Enoch Conger makes a bargain with a fish-woman on Devil's Reef and becomes increasingly aquatic, in the manner of the cursed Marsh family of "The Shadow over Innsmouth."

8. "Witches' Hollow," in *Dark Mind, Dark Heart*. Wisc.: Arkham House, 1962.

9. "The Horror from the Middle Span," in *Travellers by Night*. Wisc.: Arkham House, 1967.

10. "The Watchers out of Time," in *The Watchers Out of Time and Others*. Wisc.: Arkham House, 1972.

11. "Innsmouth Clay," in *The Watcher Out of Time and Others*. Wisc.: Arkham House, 1972.

By Zealia Bishop (Revised by H.P. Lovecraft)

Miss Bishop, Midwestern true confessions writer, used Lovecraft as a ghostwriter for horror tales, and what emerged was apparently mostly Lovecraft.

1. "The Curse of Yig." *Weird Tales*, November 1929.

Walker Davis, who is mortally afraid of snakes, and his pregnant wife travel to desert country where they hear of Yig, an Indian snake god. Both Davis and his wife are fearful. The wife sees Yig approach them at night and attacks him, but kills her husband instead. Only the baby survives this night horror, and it is kept as an amphibious creature in a zoo.

2. "Medusa's Coil." *Weird Tales*, January 1939.

De Russey brings a beautiful French wife home to Lousiana. Unfortunately, she has been a member of a strange cult. Her hair seems alive, and when her husband kills her, the hair takes on a life of its own.

3. "The Mound." *Weird Tales*, November 1940.

Locals report periodically seeing two ghostly figures atop an Indian burial mound, one an Indian of some unknown tribe or origin and the other a headless woman surrounded by blue flame. Investigators visit the mound but are never seen again. Then the narrator, an archaeologist, commences to dig into the mound, discovers an ancient manuscript, and meets a terrible fate.

By Hazel Heald (Revised by H.P. Lovecraft)

1. "The Man of Stone." *Wonder Stories*, October 1932.

Statues of a man and dog stand near a cave. A hillbilly uses a spell from the *Book of Eibon* to punish his adulterous wife and her lover.

2. "The Horror in the Museum." *Weird Tales*, July 1933.

At a London wax museum, a horrible replica of one of the Old Ones is exhibited, cradling the wax corpse of the man who discovered it.

3. "Out of the Eons." *Weird Tales*, April 1935.

The mummified body of an ancient occultist is recovered from the sea and taken to the Cabot Museum. The occultist became mummified by looking at the face of the devil-god Ghatanothoa. The mummy's brain still lives, however, and on its retina is an image of Ghatanothoa, which still has the power to petrify.

By Brian Lumley (Revised by H.P. Lovecraft)

1. "The Diary of Alonzo Typer." *Weird Tales*, February 1938.

Alonzo Typer moves into the upstate New York house of a long-deceased magician and finds horror behind a locked iron door in the cellar.

By Frank Belknap Long

1. "The Space Eaters." *Weird Tales*, July 1928.

Howard (a character based on H.P. Lovecraft) and the narrator investigate a forest where creatures from another dimension are sucking out human brains. They suck out Howard's brain.

2. "The Hounds of Tindalos." *Weird Tales*, March 1929.

Chalmers acquires a Chinese drug that allows him to journey back in time. The Hounds of Tindalos pursue him back to the present. Being angular, however, they can exist only in angular space and are repelled by curves.

3. "The Horror from the Hills." Two-part serial. *Weird Tales*, January and February 1931.

Ulman delivers Chaugnar, a stone statue of the ultimate god of good and evil, to Algernon Harris, curator of archeology at the Manhattan Museum. Ulman tells Harris that Chaugnar was given to him by some unknown Asiatic culture. Ulman is soon killed. Harris and an occultist discover that Chaugnar is not a god but a murderous being from another dimension.

4. "When Chaugnar Wakes." Poem. *Weird Tales*, September 1932.

This poem concerns the statue introduced in "The Horror from the Hills."

By Robert E. Howard

1. "The Shadow Kingdom." *Weird Tales*, August 1929.

King Kull of Valusia fights for his kingdom against a race of serpent people.

2. "The Children of the Night." *Weird Tales*, April–May 1931.

A man experiences memories of a former life when he opposed the Children of the Night, a race of half-human beings.

3. "The Black Stone." *Weird Tales*, November 1931.

The Black Stone, a monolith reputedly associated with past supernatural events, stands in a Hungarian valley. The narrator goes to the stone on Midsummer Night and sees reenacted sacrifices to a horrible toadlike god.

4. "The Thing on the Roof." *Weird Tales*, February 1932.

Tussman, a lifelong student of the occult, acquires from the narrator a first edition of the Black Book and makes a return trip to Mexico as a result. There he enters the Temple of the Toad and unwittingly frees a hoofed creature that follows him back to England and crushes his head. In this tale Howard refers to another of his Mythos stories, "The Black Stone."

5. "Arkham." Poem. *Weird Tales*, August 1932.

This is only a four-line poem, but it captures the dread of things living behind the shadows of Arkham.

6. "The Fire of Asshurbanipal." *Weird Tales*, December 1936.

Steve Clarney and Yar Ali are captured by hostile Arabs while on expedition in Central Arabia. In the lost city for which they had been searching, Clarney and Ali discover a skeleton holding a pulsing gem. Guarding the gem, however, is something apparently horrible and unhuman.

7. "Dig Me No Grave." *Weird Tales*, February 1937.

An unpaid bond leads to resurrection of the dead.

8. "The House in the Oaks," in *Dark Things*. Wisc.: Arkham House, 1971.

By Clark Ashton Smith

1. "The Return of the Sorcerer." *Strange Tales*, September 1931.

The narrator takes a job working for Carnby, a sorcerer who has murdered his brother, also a powerful sorcerer. The murdered brother returns. The *Necronomicon* is featured.

2. "The Tale of Satampra Zeiros." *Weird Tales*, November 1931.

Satampra Zeiros and Tirouv Ompallios try to rob the tomb of a king in a deserted Hyperborean city. When they violate the temple of Tsathoggua, they pay the price of disturbing a Lovecraftian Old One.

3. "The Door to Saturn." *Strange Stories*, January 1932.

Eibon, a sorcerer, flees the threat of Morghi, another sorcerer, by going to another dimension. When Morghi follows, they find themselves on Saturn in the presence of gods and natives.

4. "The Nameless Offspring." *Strange Tales*, June 1932.

Lady Agatha Tremoth is buried alive and rescued by a white thing that vanishes after the rescue. Nine months later she gives birth to a monstrous child. Sir John Tremoth's death 20 years later precipitates the escape of Lady Agatha's now-grown offspring.

5. "Ubbo-Sathla." *Weird Tales*, July 1933.

Occultist Paul Tregardis uses the crystal of a Hyperborean sorcerer to return to Hyperborea where he and the sorcerer are merged into the form of an amoebic monstrosity.

6. "The Holiness of Azedarac." *Weird Tales*, November 1933.

To escape the wrath of the Spanish Inquisition, sorcerer Azedarac banishes his accuser, monk Ambrose, back to the days of the Druids. There, a sorceress saves Ambose from sacrifice and demonstrates her own knowledge of time travel.

7. "The Seven Geases." *Weird Tales*, October 1934.

When Ralobar Vooz interrupts a spell being cast by the great magician Exdagor, the offended one puts a "gease" on Vooz, meaning that he must present himself for sacrifice to the god Tsathogguah. Tsathogguah, who has just eaten, passes the hapless Vooz on to a series of other gods and entities who also have no use for him.

8. "The Coming of the White Worm." *Stirring Science Stories*, April 1941.

In Hyperborea, the White Worm lives on an iceberg and freezes humanity as it travels. It likes to have priests as worshippers and traveling companions, and the warlock Evagh is chosen to accompany the Worm. Evagh discovers that there is a high price to be paid for having been chosen.

By August Derleth and Mark Shorer

1. "Lair of the Star-Spawn." *Weird Tales*, August 1932.

2. "Spawn of the Maelstrom." *Weird Tales*, September 1939.

An incarnation of cosmic evil dwells on the otherwise deserted island of Vomma. It radiates cold and can possess human bodies. The only defense against it is a stone pentagram.

3. "The Horror from the Depths. *Strange Stories,* October 1940.

Deep sea dredging frees the Evil Ones, who can be temporarily restrained, but not destroyed, by stone pentagrams. The survival of humanity depends on the return of the Elder Gods.

By August Derleth

1. "The Thing That Walked on the Wind." *Strange Tales*, January 1933.

A wind-walking elemental claims sacrificial victims in the Canadian wilderness. This is reminiscent not only of Lovecraft but of Algernon Blackwood's "Wendigo."

2. "The Return of Hastur." *Weird Tales*, March 1939.

When Paul Tuttle inherits the Arkham estate of his brother Amos, he finds a provision in the will instructing him to destroy all of his brother's books. He resists the provision and discovers that his brother, a sorcerer, had entered into a covenant with the god Hastur.

3. "The Sandwin Compact." *Weird Tales*, November 1940.

David visits his cousins, the Sandwins, and finds that old Sandwin has that fishy Innsmouth appearance. Old Sandwin and his ancestors have entered into a covenant with the fish god, but he now wants to break the compact in order to save his son.

4. "Ithaqua." *Strange Stories*, February 1941.

This is partly a sequel to Derleth's "Thing That Walked on the Wind."

5. "Beyond the Threshold." *Weird Tales*, September 1941.

The narrator's grandfather investigates Innsmouth and other forbidding things. He is carried off by the entity Ithaqua.

6. "The Trail of Cthulhu." *Weird Tales*, March 1944.

Andrew Phelan becomes the assistant of Dr. Laban, an Arkham folklorist. He soon finds that Laban is struggling to keep the great god Cthulhu from returning to Earth. Laban becomes involved in the struggle and realizes that he is in great danger.

7. "The Dweller in Darkness." *Weird Tales*, November 1944.

Lumberjacks try to work a camp haunted by the Old Ones. Lovecraft's Nyarlathotep makes an appearance.

8. "The Watcher from the Sky." *Weird Tales*, July 1945.

Phelan and Keene pose as Innsmouth natives in order to destroy the Cthulhu cult thriving there. They a re opposed by Abel Marsh, head of the Esoteric Order of Dagon, who also turns out to be one of the Batrachian Deep Ones.

9. "Something in Wood." *Weird Tales*, March 1948.

Jason Wecter, a collector of primitive art, acquires an interesting piece that soon leads him to fall prey to Cthulhu.

10. "The Whippoorwills in the Hills." *Weird Tales*, September 1948.

Whippoorwills constantly chirp at the Dunwich estate Dan Harrop has inherited from his brother, a sorcerer. Soon Harrop is possessed, believing himself chosen by the Old Ones.

11. "The Testament of Claiborne Boyd." *Weird Tales*, March 1949.

After Claiborne Boyd inherits his uncle's papers and art collection, he soon finds himself on route to South America with Dr. Shrewsbury to destroy a Cthulhu cult.

12. "Something from out There." *Weird Tales*, January 1951.

Three students accidentally stumble on a strange piece of occult lore, which leads them to an ancient priory and into battle against a creature from beyond the stars. This is the only such tale that Derleth never included in one of his many short story collections.

13. "The Keeper of the Key." *Weird Tales*, May 1951.

Nayland Colum, author of supernatural fiction, joins forces with Dr. Shrewsbury in an attempt to resurrect the body of Abdul Alhazred in Central America. Their goal is to discover where Cthulhu rests and then slay the creature.

14. "The Black Island." *Weird Tales*, January 1952.

Dr. Shrewsbury returns, this time in league with the United States armed forces in an attempt to locate the Black Island where Cthulhu rests. U.S. forces find the creature and resort to a hydrogen bomb in an attempt to destroy it.

15. "The House in the Valley." *Weird Tales*, July 1953.

Perkins rents the old Bishop house near Arkham and discovers that the previous owners had been sorcerers involved in cattle killing and other forbidden practices. After discovering secret tunnels under the house, Perkins falls prey to the Great Ones.

16. "The Seal of R'lyeh." *Fantastic Universe*, July 1957.

Phillips inherits his deceased uncle's house and is drawn into the cult of the Great Ones.

By Robert Bloch

1. "The Secret in the Tomb." *Weird Tales*, May 1935.

2. "The Suicide in the Study." *Weird Tales*, June 1935.

3. "The Shambler from the Stars." *Weird Tales*, September 1935.

The narrator and his friend (a character based on H.P. Lovecraft) conjure a creature that kills the friend and threatens to return for the narrator.

4. "The Mannikin." *Weird Tales*, April 1936.

An undeveloped Siamese twin is a demon.

5. "The Faceless God." *Weird Tales*, May 1936.

A ruthless doctor uncovers a statue in the Egyptian desert and discovers that it is a living form of Nyarlathotep.

6. "The Grinning Ghoul." *Weird Tales*, June 1936.

Ghouls and underground horrors.

7. "The Dark Demon." *Weird Tales*, November 1936.

A character based on H.P. Lovecraft has recurrent dreams about the Dark One. In the meantime, he turns the dreams into commercial stories. In time, Nyarlathotep comes for the author.

8. "The Secret of Sebek." *Weird Tales*, November 1937.

While attending Mardi Gras, the narrator meets a scholar who owns a mummy of a priest of Sebek. Sebek, who protects his priests, also attends Mardi Gras. Bloch followed this with a sequel unlisted by Carter titled "The Eyes of the Mummy" (*Weird Tales*, 1938).

9. "Fane of the Black Pharaoh." *Weird Tales*, December 1937.

10. "The Shadow from the Steeple." *Weird Tales*, September 1950.

This is a sequel to Lovecraft's "Haunter of the Dark." Lovecraft based his lead character in the original story on Robert Bloch. In this sequel, Blake's friend further investigates Blake's death and soon faces Nyarlathotep.

11. Notebook Found in a Deserted House." *Weird Tales*, May 1951.

By Henry Hasse

1. "The Guardian of the Book." *Weird Tales*, March 1937.

By Henry Kuttner

1. "The Salem Horror." *Weird Tales*, May 1937.

When Carson hears strange sounds in the basement of his rented house, he attributes them to rats. But the house, once owned by Salem witch Abbie Prinn, has a gruesome surprise in store for him.

2. "The Invaders." *Strange Stories*, February 1939.

3. "Hydra." *Weird Tales*, April 1939.

4. "The Hunt." *Strange Tales*, June 1939

By Ramsey Campbell

1. "The Church in High Street," in *Dark Mind, Dark Heart*. Wisc.: Arkham House, 1962.

2. "The Room in the Castle," in *The Inhabitant of the Lake and Less Welcome Tenants*. Wisc.: Arkham House, 1964.

3. "The Horror from the Bridge," in *The Inhabitant of the Lake and Less Welcome Tenants*. Wisc.: Arkham House, 1964.

4. "The Insects from Shaggai," in *The Inhabitant of the Lake and Less Welcome Tenants*. Wisc.: Arkham House, 1964.

5. "The Plain of Sound," in *The Inhabitant of the Lake and Less Welcome Tenants*. Wisc.: Arkham House, 1964.

6. "The Mine on Yuggoth," in *The Inhabitant of the Lake and Less Welcome Tenants*. Wisc.: Arkham House, 1964.

7. "The Moon-Lens," in *The Inhabitant of the Lake and Less Welcome Tenants*. Wisc.: Arkham House, 1964.

8. "The Stone on the Island," in *The Inhabitant of the Lake and Less Welcome Tenants*. Wisc.: Arkham House, 1964.

9. "Cold Print," in *Tales of the Cthulhu Mythos*. Wisc.: Arkham House, 1969.

By Vernon Shea

1. "The Haunter of the Graveyard," in *Tales of the Cthulhu Mythos*. Wisc.: Arkham House, 1969.

Television horror film host Elmer Harrod rents a house near an eerie cemetery. He discovers a flight of steps hidden there and ends up as a barely recognizable corpse.

By Brian Lumley

1. "The Sister City," in *Tales of the Cthulhu Mythos*. Wisc.: Arkham House, 1969.

2. "Cement Surroundings," in *Tales of the Cthulhu Mythos*. Wisc.: Arkham House, 1969.

3. "Billy's Oak." *The Arkham Collector*, #6, Winter 1970.

4. "An Item of Supporting Evidence." *The Arkham Collector*, #7, summer 1970.

By James Wade

1. "The Deep Ones," in *Tales of the Cthulhu Mythos*. Wisc.: Arkham House, 1969.

By Colin Wilson

1. "The Return of Lloigor," in *Tales of the Cthulhu Mythos*. Wisc.: Arkham House, 1969.

By Gary Myers

1. "The House of the Worm." *The Arkham Collector*, #7, summer 1970.

2. "Yokh the Necromancer." *The Arkham Collector*, #8, winter 1971.

3. "Passing of a Dreamer." *The Arkham Collector*, #9, spring 1971.

By Lin Carter

1. "The Doom of Yakthoob." *The Arkham Collector*, #10, summer 1971.

2. "Shaggai," in *Dark Things*. Wisc.: Arkham House, 1971.

Carter lists six more of his stories scheduled for publication in *The Arkham Collector* after 1971.

PART THREE

Films Based on Lovecraft's Works

The following is a filmography of motion pictures that credit Lovecraft or are identifiably adapted from his works.

The Haunted Palace (1963)
American International, U.S.A.

Directed and produced by Roger Corman. Screenplay by Charles Beaumont, based on *The Case of Charles Dexter Ward* by H.P. Lovecraft and "The Haunted Palace" by Edgar Allan Poe. Cinematography by Floyd Crosby. Art direction by Daniel Haller. Music by Ronald Stein. Set decoration by Harry Reif. Edited by Ronald Sinclair. 85 minutes.

Cast: Vincent Price (Joseph Curwen and Charles Dexter Ward), Debra Paget (Ann Ward), Lon Chaney, Jr. (Simon Orne), Frank Maxwell (Dr. Willet), Leo Gordon (Weeden), Elisha Cook (Smith), John Dierkes (West), Milton Parsons (Jabez Hutchinson), Cathy Merchant (Hester Tillinghast), Guy Wilkerson (Leach), Harry Ellerbe (minister), I. Stanford Jolley (Mr. Carmody), Darlene Lucht (young woman victim), Barboura Morris (Mrs. Weeden), and Bruno Ve Sota (bartender).

Synopsis

In the New England fishing village of Arkham, in the year 1765, the villagers are aware and fearful of strange events taking place at the palacial mansion of Joseph Curwen. One night they follow a young woman who walks as though in a trance to the mansion, where she participates in strange rites performed by Curwen from an occult text, *The Necronomicon.* Curwen is a sorcerer who imprisons young girls from the village and sacrifices them to creatures from another dimension.

Unwilling to put up with such activities in their midst, the villagers question Curwen and his woman, Hester Tillinghast. When Curwen dodges their questions, the frustrated villagers seize Curwen, tie him to a tree, and burn him alive as a warlock. Before dying, however, he curses the villagers, their children and their children's children, and vows to return from the dead.

Over a century later, Charles Dexter Ward and his wife Ann arrive in Arkham by ship. When the descendants of the villagers who burned Curwen notice that Ward, an admitted descendant of Curwen, bears a striking resemblance to the deceased warlock, they display hostility. Indeed, they fear that Curwen's curse has been fulfilled and that they will soon die. As the Wards are on their way to take possession of the Curwen mansion, they encounter strangely deformed men, women and children in the streets of Arkham.

Inside the mansion, the Wards discover a painting of Joseph Curwen and notice its amazing resemblance to Charles. They also meet Simon Orne, who identifies himself as the caretaker and seems strangely familiar to Ward. When Ward looks again at the portrait, his personality and appearance change to resemble that of the warlock. From that time on, Ward wages a battle for his own soul but is often possessed by Curwen's more powerful spirit. Ward/Curwen is soon plotting with Orne and a warlock named Jabez Hutchinson to restore Curwen to full power. These changes, of course, dismay Ann, who loves her husband and does not understand what is going on.

It seems that the mutants in the village were the results of the strange mating rites conducted by Curwen a century ago, as well as part of the fulfillment of his curse. The curse continues to fruition as several of the villagers are hideously burned to death. One night while

Curwen has taken over Ward, Orne and Hutchinson unearth Hester Tillinghast's coffin and prepare to resurrect her.

By this time, the villagers decide that they must do what their ancestors did a century ago — destroy the warlock to save themselves. As Ward/Curwen is about to sacrifice Ann to a horrible creature conjured from a pit, the villagers storm the mansion and set it afire. The villagers rescue Ann, and Ward staggers out of the flaming house, apparently free of Curwen's power. Or is he? As they watch the mansion perish, Charles' and Ann's faces seem to resemble those of Curwen and Hester:

> While, like a rapid, ghastly river,
> Through the pale door,
> A hideous throng rush out forever,
> And laugh — but smile no more
> — Edgar Allan Poe

Adaptation

Although *The Haunted Palace* is advertised as the sixth Edgar Allan Poe adaptation directed by Roger Corman, it is actually based on Lovecraft's "Case of Charles Dexter Ward," in which eighteenth-century magician Joseph Curwen settles in the New World to carry out his experiments in necromancy and eternal life. Neighbors become frightened by his exploits and execute him. In the twentieth century, Curwen's distant descendant, Charles Dexter Ward, discovers that Curwen's associates are still attempting their experiments in Europe. Disaster results when Ward attempts to follow in Curwen's footsteps.

"I fought against calling it a Poe film," Corman said, "but AIP had made so much money with Poe films that they just stuck his name on it for box office appeal."* At least Lovecraft is acknowledged in the film credits.

As one can easily see, the film follows the general line of the novella. The key Lovecraftian theme most adequately addressed in the film is that of humanity's cosmic insignificance. To that end, the film introduces audiences to *The Necronomicon*, a book capable of summoning such gods (or extraterrestrials) as Cthulhu and Yog-Sothoth, both of whom are indifferent to the fate of humanity. As Ward/Curwen

*Ed Naha. *Horror from Screen to Scream*. New York: Avon, 1975, p. 233.

admits in the film, he simply obeys these powers; he cannot understand them.

At one point in the film, Dr. Willett explains to the Wards the legend of "the Elder Gods, the Dark Ones from beyond who had once ruled the world ... but now are merely waiting for an opportunity to regain that control." This line, however, is adapted from a quotation attributed to Lovecraft by the founder of Arkham House, August Derleth. Lovecraft would disavow the idea of a cosmic battle between good and evil, between the Old Ones and the Judeo-Christian god, an idea with which Derleth was comfortable. Though scholars today doubt that Lovecraft ever uttered the words attributed to him by Derleth, the latter's erroneous interpretation continues to be associated with Lovecraft.

Though in the film some deformed citizens prowl the streets of Arkham, they are nothing like the nasty supernatural offspring Lovecraft conjures in his prose.

Critique

Roger Corman (b. 1926) had directed five very successful films based loosely on the works of Poe. Vincent Price had starred in the first four and Ray Milland in the fifth. At that point, Corman wanted to adapt the story by H.P. Lovecraft to star Ray Milland as Ward/Curwen, Boris Karloff as Simon Orne, and Hazel Court as Ann Ward. Corman wanted to title the film *The Haunted Village* and bypass Vincent Price to avoid it being mistaken for another Poe film. Corman's plan fell apart, however, when AIP insisted on Price, Boris Karloff fell ill and had to be replaced by Lon Chaney, Jr., and Debra Paget replaced Hazel Court. Then, against Corman's protests, the film was released as a Poe adaptation anyway, supposedly based on the author's poem "The Haunted Palace."

Given all this confusion, the final product is quite good. Beginning with opening scenes in the fogbound New England village, Corman sustains the dark and brooding atmosphere of his earlier Poe efforts. Ronald Stein's strong musical score is as foreboding as the lightning splitting the sky above Arkham, and Daniel Haller's art direction brings the fog-shrouded village and "haunted palace" to vivid life. The cast is uniformly effective. In supporting roles, veteran character actors

Leo Gordon, Elisha Cook, and Frank Maxwell are particularly impressive. While there are numerous effective horror scenes, the most eerie is that in which Price and Paget are surrounded by mutants on a fogbound Arkham street, and Ted Coodley's realistic makeup work allows the camera some very unsettling closeups of the menacing mutants.

Corman respected the reputation of Lon Chaney, Jr., as a horror man and used him accordingly. Early in the film, Paget, in closeup, is exploring a room of the mansion when she is shocked by a collision with Chaney. Later, Corman employs a similar technique as Price, in closeup, backs into Chaney, who is merely offering him his coat. Finally, Chaney emerges from the shadows to frighten the terrified Paget into a faint as she is making her way through the palace dungeon.

The best performance in the film is that of Vincent Price, the man Corman had hoped to avoid casting for reasons other than acting ability. Price gives a nuanced performance with no hint of the self-parody many critics accuse him of. Actually, Price's serious work displays little of such over-the-top acting; his critics must be watching other films.

Interestingly, *The Haunted Palace* is the only "Poe" film by Corman in which evil (in human terms) ultimately emerges victorious. This is, of course, more the influence of Lovecraft than of Poe.

Rating: 2½

Die, Monster, Die! (1965)
aka *Monster of Terror*
American International, U. S. A. and Great Britain

Directed by Daniel Haller. Produced by Pat Green. Executive Producers, James H. Nicholson and Samuel Z. Arkoff. Screenplay by Jerry Sohl, from "The Colour Out of Space" by H.P. Lovecraft. Music composed by Don Banks. Musical Direction by Philip Martell. Continuity by Tilly Day. Cinematography by Paul Beeson. Art Direction by Colin Southcott; Make-up by Jimmy Evans; Edited by Alfred Cox. Hairdresser, Bobbie Smith. 80 minutes

Cast: Boris Karloff (Nahum Witley), Nick Adams (Stephen Reinhart), Freda Jackson (Letitia Witley), Suzan Farmer (Susan Witley),

Terence De Marney (Merwyn), Patrick Magee (Dr. Henderson), Paul Farrell (Jason), George Moon (cab driver), Gretchen Franklin (Miss Bailey), Sydney Bromley (Pierce), Billy Milton (Henry).

Synopsis

A young American scientist, Stephen Reinhart, visits England to reunite with his fiancée Susan and meet her parents, Nahum and Letitia Witley. Nahum, a bitter old man confined to a wheelchair, asks Stephen to leave. Stephen refuses and meets Susan's mother, a bedridden phantom who, speaking from behind a heavy black veil, also begs Stephen to leave. Stephen ignores all requests for him to leave and remains at Susan's invitation.

Nahum and his manservant Merwyn make frequent trips to a room in the basement where an unearthly green light glows. Letitia pleads with Nahum to let Susan leave with Stephen, but Nahum argues that the idea is ridiculous. Letitia then unveils her hideously disfigured, fungus-covered face.

Stephen discovers in the library a book that belonged to Susan's grandfather, Corbin Witley. From it he learns that a rock from outer space fell on the Witley property and showed signs of producing giant plant life. But the rock brought with it a curse. All who encounter it are eventually transformed and go mad. The dark force from outer space is preying on the Witleys.

Stephen tries to get information from Dr. Henderson, the village physician, but the alcoholic doctor has seen too much at the Witley place and will not cooperate. When Stephen returns, he is attacked by a black-robed figure, but escapes. Merwyn dies. Stephen tries to get Susan out of the house, but they are drawn to the greenhouse where they discover glowing green crystals that make normal plants and animals mutate.

A storm rises. Letitia dies, crazed, hideous, and homicidal. Before he can destroy it, the giant green crystal in the cellar turns Nahum into a glowing monster. He is destroyed while pursuing Stephen and Susan. The house bursts into flames, and the lovers flee to freedom.

Adaptation

Though Jerry Sohl's screenplay credits Lovecraft's "The Colour Out of Space," it owes as much, if not more, to American International's

Corman-Poe series, particularly *The Fall of the House of Usher* (1960). As I will explain later, the parallels are striking.

As with Corman's *Haunted Palace*, Lovecraft must share credit with Poe, one of his obvious literary inspirations. In this case Sohl takes a Lovecraft science fiction tale with little, if any, Poe influence, changes the setting from New England to Great Britain, and writes what is largely a remake of Corman's *House of Usher*.

So, how much does *Die, Monster, Die!* owe to H.P. Lovecraft? Certainly enough to assign the credit. Early in the story we read:

> When I went into the hills and vales to survey for the new reservoir they told me the place was evil. They told me this is Arkham, and because that is a very old town full of witch legends I thought the evil must be something which grand-dams had whispered to children through the centuries.... Then I saw that dark westward tangle of glens and slopes for myself, and ceased to wonder at anything besides its own elder mystery. It was morning when I saw it, but shadows lurked always there.... Weeds and briers reigned, and furtive wild things rustled in the undergrowth. Upon everything was a haze of restlessness and oppression; a touch of the unreal and the grotesque, as if some vital element of perspective or chiaroscuro were awry.

But this is nothing to what the narrator experiences on the blasted heath: "five acres of grey desolation" that appeared overcome in the past by a fire. The narrator passes the ruins of a chimney, a cellar, and "the yawning black maw of an abandoned well whose stagnant vapours played strange tricks with the hues of the sunlight." When he inquires in the village about the place, the residents whisper about something that happened in the "strange days" but refuse or are unable to explain further.

The film's blasted heath doesn't live up to Lovecraft's description. Fog creeps over the land, but otherwise we see only charred twigs and branches that crumble in Stephen's grasp. There is also greenery in the film's landscape, which counters any suggestion of catastrophe.

In Haller's film, Stephen arrives in Arkham and is rudely treated by villagers who will not help him reach the old Witley Place. Though this echoes Lovecraft's story, it owes more to the typical scenes of frightened villagers that we see in many films from *Dracula* (1931) to Corman's *Haunted Palace* (1963).

In Lovecraft's story, the narrator pieces together events that happened in the "strange days" with the help of Ammi, a farmer who tells of the fate that befell the Nahum Gardner family after a stone from outer space struck their property. Screenwriter Sohl allows Nahum his first name from the story but changes the last name to Witley, possibly a variation on the name Whately from Lovecraft's "Dunwich Horror." In *Die, Monster, Die!* Stephen witnesses what happens firsthand, and the alcoholic Dr. Henderson, to whom he turns for information, is singularly uncooperative — certainly not based on the story's helpful Ammi.

Merwin, Nahum's son in the Lovecraft story, becomes Merwyn the servant in the film. Both die as a result of evil force. The film's injection of Nahum's late father as a black magician involved with dark forces from outer space seems lifted from such Lovecraftian works as *The Case of Charles Dexter Ward*.

In both story and film, plant and animal mutations abound. Also in both story and film, Nahum observes the deadly effect visited on his family and himself but refuses or is unable to leave or seek help. In the story, Nahum's wife Nabby mutates until Nahum locks her in an attic room. When Ammi finds her, it is the most terrifying part in Lovecraft's story and one of the most disturbing sequences in his entire corpus. Lovecraft elicits this terror through suggestion:

> It was quite dark inside, for the window was small and half-obscured by the crude wooden bars; and Ammi could see nothing at all on the wide-planked floor. The stench was beyond enduring, and before proceeding further he had to retreat to another room and return with his lungs filled with breathable air. When he did enter he saw something dark in the corner, and upon seeing it more clearly he screamed outright. While he screamed he thought a momentary cloud eclipsed the window, and a second later he felt himself brushed as if by some hateful current of vapour. Strange colours danced before his eyes; and had not a present horror numbed him he would have thought of the globule in the meteor that the geologists *[sic]* hammer had shattered, and of the morbid vegetation that had sprouted in the spring. As it was he thought only of the

blasphemous monstrosity which confronted him, and which all too clearly had shared the nameless fate of young Thaddeus and the livestock. But the terrible thing about this horror was that it very slowly and perceptibly moved as it continued to crumble.

How Ammi destroys the abomination is left to our imagination as the narrator reports that

There are things that cannot be mentioned, and what is done in common humanity is something cruelly judged by the law. I gathered that no moving thing was left in that attic room, and that to leave anything capable of motion there would have been a deed so monstrous as to damn any accountable being to eternal torment.

Lovecraft tells us shortly thereafter that "... Ammi's grip tightened on a heavy stick he had picked up in the attic for some purpose."

Casting aside suggestion and mood, the film's Letitia is just another hideous monster run amuck, less effective than mad Madeline in Corman's *Fall of the House of Usher.*

In both story and film, Nahum and his house are destroyed, though in the film, the lovers (who do not appear in the story) escape the conflagration to give audiences a happy ending.

Perhaps the most crucial thing missing in this adaptation is Lovecraft's purpose. In "The Colour out of Space," the author plays with the idea of an alien life form completely different from anything humans can imagine. In a 1916 letter he writes: "How do we know that form of molecular motion called 'life' is the highest of all forms? Perhaps the dominant creature — the most rational and God-like of all beings — is an invisible gas!" Such is the nature of the "colour" out of space, but no such radical otherness is conveyed in the film. Instead, we get what appears to be a radioactive stone of occult origin capable of contaminating the environment and the living things in it.

Critique

Art director Daniel Haller (b. 1928) was eager to break into directing, and in 1965, executive director Roger Corman gave him his chance. Haller had proven his worth as Corman's art director since 1958, often adding immensely to the success of Corman's films. At the time,

Corman was winding down his Poe series composed of *The Fall of the House of Usher* (1960), *The Pit and the Pendulum* (1961), *The Premature Burial* (1962) *Tales of Terror* (1962), *The Raven* (1963), *The Haunted Palace* (1963, actually based on Lovecraft's *Case of Charles Dexter Ward*), *The Masque of the Red Death* (1964), and *The Tomb of Ligeia* (1965). The latter two films were shot in England, as was *Die, Monster, Die!*

Haller had read Lovecraft's "Colour out of Space" and considered it a great basic story. Regardless, he followed the Corman-Poe formula and created a pale imitation of that series rather than a serious adaptation of Lovecraft. In addition to the similarities pointed out above, Haller's film jettisons the country folk of Lovecraft's story and sets events in an opulent English mansion. Haller admits that he lacked confidence in his first directorial outing and that he gave the studio what he thought it wanted.

Haller had worked with Boris Karloff (1887–1969) on several other Corman films and had little difficulty engaging the actor for *Die, Monster, Die!* Karloff, appearing in yet another horror film, reportedly held this view on typecasting: Actors are darn lucky to be typecast — like any tradesman who is known for a particular specialty. It's better than not working at all and I feel I could not have been more fortunate in my career than being type-cast as a villain. If the film's Nahum Witley had been more like the story's Nahum Gardner, Karloff's task as an actor might have been more challenging, but as it stands, Karloff's talents weren't tested. As a typecast actor he had played similar roles many times before and knew exactly how and what to deliver to add a sinister aura to proceedings. One interesting moment occurs early in the film when Stephen reveals that he and Susan met at an American university in a science class. "Science," Karloff sneers, implying through his tone that science is of little help in the world he has come to know.

Additional pressbook ballyhoo proclaimed that in *Die, Monster, Die!* "Karloff portrays a seemingly kindly elderly gentleman who becomes transformed into his new monster — a terrifying creature of sheer horror and nightmarish fright." Aside from the fact that a stunt man in a glowing, bald head-mask performs Karloff's monster scenes, the result is hardly nightmarish. In fact, Karloff's monster is a mutated human being with shining face and hands, vaguely reminiscent of his monster in *The Invisible Ray*, although there his "monster" had more motivation.

The film's obligatory love interest is provided by Nick Adams (1931–1968) and Suzan Farmer (b. 1943). Adams, best known for his starring role in the television series *The Rebel* (1959–1960) and for an Academy Award nomination for *Twilight of Honor* (1963), on several occassions expressed his love for horror films. In a pressbook quote for *Die, Monster, Die!*, he said he considered monsters "great people" and went on to explain that he "always saw them as poor, wretched ugly creatures whom nobody loved and who were persecuted for being what they couldn't help being." While the monsters Adams confronts in *Die Monster, Die!* are of this variety, they fail to elicit anything near the sympathy evoked by Boris Karloff in his famous portrayals of Franken-stein's Monster. Interestingly, the same year that Adams was born, Karloff made his debut as the Monster. As Stephen Reinhart, Adams brings an American no-nonsense, tough-minded perspective to bear on the strange occurrences at Witley Mansion. Adams would continue starring in horror and science fiction films until his death three years later of a drug overdose.

British starlet Suzan Farmer (yes, she was actually christened Suzan with a "z") made her film debut in *The Wild and the Willing* (1962), where she met her future husband, actor Ian McShane. Farmer is ade-quate as Susan Witley but never rises above the typical young female lead prevalent in horror films of the period. She would appear in other films, including Hammer's *Dracula, Prince of Darkness* (1966), but a taste for alcohol and only average talent led to her eventual retirement from the screen.

Adding additional gravitas to the film are British character actor Patrick Magee (1924–1982) and British character actress Freda Jackson (1909–1990). As the alcoholic Dr. Henderson who refuses to cooper-ate with Stephen Reinhart's search for information, Magee reveals a bit-ter man whose experiences at the Witley Mansion had so hardened him to a world bereft of God and meaning that he abandoned his practice in despair. Though Jackson does most of her acting behind a heavy black veil, her voice and physical movements are right for the role of afflicted Letitia Witley. Terence De Marney, who plays the manser-vant, is perfectly cast.

Despite turning to one of H.P. Lovecraft's best stories as a source, too much in *Die, Monster, Die!* was familiar territory to audiences in the mid-sixties. Many techniques that had been fresh once upon a time no longer worked as well. For example, the young man traveling to a shunned house to collect his fiancée, the secretive, resistant relative, the family paintings exhibited on the wall, the extended exploration of forbidding hallways and grounds by candlelight, the presence of a loyal manservant who stays on in the face of obvious danger, mad folks running amuck, and a final conflagration were all familiar devices from the Corman-Poe series, particularly from *The Fall of the House of Usher*. In addition, a large plant attacks Suzan Farmer much as a similar plant attacks actress Beverley Tyler in the Boris Karloff vehicle *Voodoo Island* (1957), and the discovery of the greenhouse mutations suggests a similar scene at the conclusion of *The Unearthly* (1957).

Jerry Sohl's screenplay is static, and Don Banks' musical score unremarkable. Regrettably, only the sets periodically suggest the considerable eeriness of Lovecraft's story. One scene, however, does stand out. As Karloff tries to destroy the glowing stone from outer space, the green from the stone creeps through his body like color coursing through a spider web.

Often double-billed in the United States with *Planet of the Vampires*, the film opened to lukewarm reviews. Mimicking baseball announcer Harey Carey's call of a home run, posters and ads for the film shouted, "It could happen! It may happen! It might happen! to you!" In addition, Boris Karloff's frightening visage appeared alongside a wielded axe and above a swooning girl under the question, "Can you face the ultimate in diabolism ... can you stand pure terror?" A Dell comic book tie-in captured more of Lovecraft's mood with these words on the cover: "An incredible force of evil strikes fear into the house at the end of the World." Perhaps the film was also helped by Lancer Books' paperback publication of *The Colour out of Space* in 1964.

Rating: 2

The Shuttered Room (1967)
aka *Blood Island*

Seven Arts, Great Britain

Produced by Philip Hazelton. Directed by David Greene. Screenplay by D.B. Dedrov and Nathaniel Tanchuck, based on the story by H.P. Lovecraft and August Derleth. Executive producer, Bernard Schwarts. Associate producer, Alexander Jacobs. Music composed and arranged by Basil Kirchin. Music conducted by Jack Nathan. Cinematography by Kenneth Hodges; Art direction by Brian Eatwell. Edited by Brian Smedley-Aston. Sound mixed by Kenneth Osborne. Makeup by Harry Frampton. 82 minutes.

Cast: Gig Young (Mike Kelton), Carol Lynley (Susannah Kelton), Oliver Reed (Ethan), Flora Robson (Aunt Agatha), William Devlin (Zebulon), Bernard Kay (Tait), Judith Arthy (Emma), Robert Cawdron (Luther), Celia Hewitt (Aunt Sarah), Ingrid Bower (village girl).

Synopsis

Mike and Susannah Kelton drive from New York to Dunwich Island, the home of Susannah's family, so that Susannah can claim the mill where she was born and reared before being sent away as a child by her aunt Agatha. Mike has visions of turning the old mill into a summer home. After crossing by ferry to the island, they are harassed by young Ethan Whateley and his band of local yokels on a joyride.

At their first stop, Mike meets Zebulon Whateley, whose foundry assistant was blinded in one eye while sleeping overnight in the mill. "There's no one but demons live there," the worker warns. Undeterred, Mike and Susannah drive on to the mill. Ethan arrives and takes the couple to see Agatha Whateley, who occupies a lighthouse. She warns Mike and Susannah to avoid the mill for their own good. Mike is not impressed by the warning and takes Susannah back to the house.

Throughout the film, someone or something peers down from the shuttered room overhanging the mill.

Later, Ethan and his gang chase and corner Susannah on a pier. She is rescued when Mike arrives and dumps Ethan into the water with a flourish of martial arts moves. Later, a local tart is murdered in the mill by the lurker in the shuttered room.

At the film's conclusion, the lurker proves to be Susannah's mad twin sister. Ethan chases Susannah but is killed by the sister in the shuttered room. As the room catches fire, Mike tries to rescue the girl but is thwarted when Aunt Agatha arrives, drags the girl back into the burning room, and locks the door from the inside. Aunt Agatha and her secret go up in flames as her pet hawk, symbolizing freedom, hovers overhead.

Adaptation

"The Shuttered Room," purported to be a fragment or outline left among Lovecraft's papers at the time of his death, was allegedly completed by August Derleth. Though it is a sequel to "The Dunwich Horror" and "The Shadow over Innsmouth," I cannot see that Lovecraft himself contributed much if any writing to the story. It is essentially Derleth's. Nevertheless, we must address it as part of the Lovecraft cinema.

In the story, Abner Whateley returns to Dunwich after pursuing his education around the world. His grandfather, Luther Whateley, has left him a mill located along the Miskatonic River. Years ago, Abner's aunt Sarah had visited kin in Innsmouth. Upon returning, she was soon locked permanently by Grandfather Whateley in the shuttered room overlooking the mill wheel. It seems that Sarah's relatives belonged to a cult called the Deep Ones, worshippers of the ancient gods Dagon and Cthulhu. These people were reputedly part human and part fish. Sarah fell in love with young Ralsa Marsh, a member of the cult, which precipitated her inprisonment in the shuttered room.

In papers left to Abner, Grandfather Whateley instructs his grandson to destroy the shuttered room and to kill everything in the room, regardless of how small and apparently insignificant. Soon cattle are mysteriously slaughtered and eaten in the area, and then a human is murdered and torn apart. Abner discovers to his horror that a small frog-like being had inhabited the room along with Aunt Sarah. When Abner broke a pane of glass freeing it, it grew in size and went prowling for food. Upon returning, it shrunk back to its normal size and hid once again in the room.

Abner is finally able to set the thing afire, at which point it struggles in the flames crying "Mama-mama." The half-frog, half-human product of Sarah and Ralsa's union is destroyed. One of the most memorable parts of the story is Derleth's unnerving description of the monster:

> There, squatting in the midst of the tumbled bedding from that long abandoned bed, sat a monstrous, leathery-skinned creature that was neither frog nor man, one gorged with food, with blood still slavering from its batrachian jaws and upon its webbed fingers — a monstrous entity that had strong, powerfully long arms, grown from its bestial body like those of a frog, and tapering off into a man's hands, save for the webbing between the fingers.

As one can easily see, the film has little to do with the story. Instead of Abner Whateley returning to the village of Dunwich, we get the Keltons visiting Dunwich Island. Though the setting is supposed to be New England, the film was shot in Great Britain. In the film, someone or something is living in the shuttered room attached to the mill, but the occupant owes more to Charlotte Brontë's *Jane Eyre* than to Lovecraft. Conflagration solves the problem in both story and film, but the similarities end there.

The real secret of the shuttered room is that the film was initially to be much different and more Lovecraftian than what finally appeared in theaters. The earlier, discarded scenario begins with Luther Whateley securely chaining someone or something, which whimpers like a child, to the wall of the grinding room in his mill and locking the door. He then hurls his young wife Sarah into an adjacent room with shuttered windows and bolts the door.

In the final version, Susannah's parents put her to bed in the mill. The room at the top of the stairs opens and someone or something walks downstairs and approaches Susannah's bed. Sensing something is wrong, Susannah's parents spring from their beds, and her father guides the intruder back into the upstairs room.

At that point, the plot lines become similar as Mike and Susannah arrive on the island and meet Ethan and Aunt Agatha. Then the original film scenario changes course again. Mike and Susannah decide to sleep in their car on the first night, during which Susannah is frightened by a hulking figure with webbed fingers and a slimy skin peering into the car. Her screams frighten it away.

Later, Mike finds an imprint of webbed hands on the mill wheel. This event, adapted from Derleth's story, never makes it into the film since the denizen of the shuttered room is no longer Derleth's "frogman" but a madwoman.

The first and final scenarios merge once again as Ethan's gang beats up Mike, and Ethan chases Susannah about the mill. Then the scenario changes again as the monster, described as "a huge, hellish figure with powerful out-stretched arms and hooded, lizard-like eyes glaring insanely," crushes Ethan to death. Mike escapes from Ethan's gang and arrives with Aunt Agatha in time to carry Susannah to safety. Villagers then arrive and in stereotypical horror film fashion drive the creature into the swamp.

Broken-hearted Aunt Agatha reveals that the monster is Jonah, Sarah's child, and pleads with the mob to spare his life. But the villagers hound the pathetic brute into the marshy bog with pitchforks until the last, heartrending cry for "Maa-maa" is cut off and he sinks into the oozing mud and slime.

The initial scenario, which would have run 100 minutes (18 minutes longer than the actual final product) is obviously far superior in conception. The controversial director Ken Russell, who was first tapped to direct the film, deserted the project and left it for former actor and successful television director David Greene. Greene took the script unread and soon became quite dissatisfied with his decision. As shooting began, Greene practically rewrote the script day by day. According to Carol Lynley (in an interview with me), Greene allowed Oliver Reed and her to rewrite and ad-lib scenes.

Critique

As it stands, *The Shuttered Room* is a dull disappointment. American light comedy leading man Gig Young (1913–1978) had earned Academy Award nominations for performances in *Come Fill the Cup* (1951) and *Teacher's Pet* (1958), and he would take home an Oscar for his performance in *They Shoot Horses, Don't They?* (1969). But he irritatingly smirks throughout *The Shuttered Room* and does not make a very sympathetic male lead. In 1978, he committed suicide after murdering his fifth wife.

American leading lady Carol Lynley (b. 1942) had been a success on both stage and screen before entering the strange world of Derleth and Lovecraft, her most memorable films being *Blue Denim* (1959) and *Bunny Lake Is Missing* (1965). In *The Shuttered Room*, Lynley is appropriately fragile and vulnerable. She also does a commendable job doubling briefly as her mad twin sister.

Burly Brit Oliver Reed (1938–1999) excelled in bully-boy roles, and he has a juicy one in *The Shuttered Room*. Whether running angrily across the countryside, attempting to beat up Gig Young, driving his truck headlong into a stack of empty oil drums, rape-chasing Carol Lynley, or falling into the muddy waters of the Great Stour River, Reed energetically rises to the physical occasion. But he is more than just a physical presence; he employs impertinent humor or dark sullenness to steal every scene he is in. After starring impressively in such films as *The Curse of the Werewolf* (1961), *The Damned* (1962), *The Joker* (1966), *Oliver!* (1968), *Women in Love* (1969), *The Devils* (1971), and *The Triple Echo* (1972, probably his best performance), a lifetime of hard drinking ended both his career and his life during the production of *Gladiator* (1999).

Distinguished British stage actress Dame Flora Robson (1902–1984) delivers the best performance in the film as strong-willed Aunt Agatha. Yes, she is strong, but she is touching when called upon to reflect deep sadness and resignation. When the film is over, Robson's performance is the most memorable.

The screenplay is most responsible for the film's failure. Not only would it have been much more effective had it remained unchanged from its original conception, but in its final form it could have been improved with better pacing. We are subjected to too many scenes that if shortened might have produced suspense and moved the film along at an exciting pace. Instead we watch Carol Lynley slowly walking around, dusting the mill, and running (for what seems forever) across the countryside. We see Gig Young driving his T-Bird, and we see people being watched — but despite all of this time consuming activity, the plot is not advanced. What starts as a promising film deteriorates into a bore about a third of the way through. Even the two murders that occur are relatively unengaging and poorly handled — which leads us to the director.

British director David Greene (b. 1921) commands a hand-held camera to occasional good effect in breaking the monotony, includes many subjective camera shots from the shuttered room to suggest a menacing presence, and gets good performances out of most actors involved. He could have executed the murder scenes more artfully and suspensefully, but that alone would not have saved the production.

One final flaw is Basil Kirchin's musical score. Getting off on the wrong foot, Kirchin destroys any dark mood with the brassy opening theme. From there on, things don't improve as the music continues to work against the mood.

Advertising for the film was as dull as the film itself. Some newspaper ads featured a cowering woman above the words, "There are some doors that should never be opened...." Other ads used the same words beside an unrecognizable Oliver Reed struggling with an unrecognizable Carol Lynley. Another catch-line is the none-too-original "Sleep one night in the house with the shuttered room and you may never want to sleep again." Or how about the poetic "Close the Doors. Nail the Beams. What's Inside Must Never Be Seen!"

One ad proclaims, "The new shocker is based on a short story by H.P. Lovecraft, an American writer whose tales of horror, murder and suspense are generally conceded to be the successors to those of Edgar Allan Poe." At least that statement might be reasonably defended.

Interestingly, Dell published a paperback tie-in by Julia Withers, not the original *The Shuttered Room and Other Pieces by H.P. Lovecraft and Divers Hands.* The original story may have been deemed too far removed from the film to serve as an effective tie-in; or maybe Dell could not get the publishing rights. Without access to Withers' rare paperback, it is impossible to say which scenario it adapted.

Rating: 1½

Curse of the Crimson Altar (1968)
aka *The Crimson Cult*, aka *Crimson Altar*, aka *The Reincarnation*, aka *Spirit of the Dead*, aka *Witch House*

Tigon and American International
(Great Britain and U.S.A.)

Directed by Vernon Sewell. Produced by Louis M. Heyward. Executive producer, Tony Tenser. Screenplay by Mervyn Haisman and Henry Lincoln, based on "The Dreams in the Witch House" by H.P. Lovecraft. Associate producer, Gerry Levy. Cinematography by Johnny Coquillon. Art direction by Derek Barrington. Edited by Howard Lanning. Music composed and conducted by Peter Knight. Makeup by Pauline Worden and Elizabeth Blatin. 87 minutes

Cast: Boris Karloff (Professor Marshe), Christopher Lee (Morley), Mark Eden (Robert Manning), Virginia Wetherell (Eve), Barbara Steele (Lavinia), Michael Gough (Elder), Rupert Davies (Dr. Radford), Rosemarie Reede (Esther), Derek Tansley (judge), Michael Warren (chauffeur), Ron Pember (petrol attendant), Denys Peek (Peter Manning), Nicholas Head (blacksmith), Nita Lorraine (woman with whip), Carol Anne (first virgin), Jenny Shaw (second virgin), Vivienne Carlton (sacrifice victim), Roger Avon (Sgt. Tyson).

Synopsis

Antique dealer Robert Manning travels to Greymarsh Lodge to locate his missing brother Peter, who vanished after sending a collectible candlestick and letter from the lodge. The lodge's owner, Mr. Morley, claims never to have seen or heard of Peter Manning, but since the countryside is observing the annual celebration of the burning of Lavinia, the Black Witch, Morley invites Robert to stay. The witch, who was burned about 300 years earlier, was a Morley, an ancestor of the lodge owner.

A sinister gentleman in a wheelchair, Professor Marshe, arrives and relates that Lavinia, before dying, cursed those responsible for her death. Since then, many descendants of those responsible have died horribly and mysteriously. Professor Marshe should know, as he is one of the world's leading experts on witchcraft and a collector of torture instruments.

Robert attends the ceremony commemorating the burning with Morley's beautiful niece Eve, who works as Professor Marshe's private secretary. Marshe follows them and watches with growing agitation.

Robert describes Peter to Eve, who says that Peter was definitely in the lodge a short time ago, though he did not go by that name. Convinced that something is awry, Robert goes to the graveyard and finds Morley and Marshe among the stones. They invite him to the lodge for a brandy, at which point Morley recalls the person Robert describes as his brother, though he too claims that the man did not go by the name of Peter.

Later, Robert dreams that he is in a room surrounded by practitioners of the black arts. Present are Lavinia, a strange woman with a whip, a man wearing antlers, the butler Elder, and Peter Manning. Lavinia insists that Robert sign "the Book." When he refuses, she lunges at him with a bodkin (used by witch hunters). When Robert awakens, he wonders if his experience was a dream or reality.

The next day, Robert finds blood in his room and discovers a secret room that he recognizes as the one in his dream. Eve accompanies him into the room, which appears not to have been used for years. Robert discovers, however, that the spider webs are artificial. Eve, as puzzled as Robert, denies any knowledge of the room.

Investigating for herself, Eve learns from Dr. Radford, the village parson, that the Mannings are the last remaining relatives of those who burned Lavinia. She recognizes other names of relatives who stayed at the lodge and soon died. Has Peter been killed, and is Robert next? Frightened, Eve returns to the lodge only to discover that her uncle knows what she has been up to. Soon she finds herself hypnotized on an altar in the witch room. Sitting near her is Robert, strapped to a chair.

Just as Morley is about to sacrifice Eve, a shot rings out and Morley drops the knife. Standing in the doorway is Professor Marshe with a pistol. The witch room is set ablaze and Professor Marshe and his servant free Eve and Robert. The police and firemen arrive in time to see Morley trapped on the roof by the flames. Dr. Marshe explains that he suspected Morley of getting revenge on behalf of his relative, the

Black Witch. As Marshe, Robert and Eve watch, Morley turns into the laughing apparition of Lavinia surrounded by flames. Then he dies.

Adaptation

Lovecraft's "Dreams in the Witch House" is not a favorite of scholars, most of whom consider it an unsatisfying read. Many readers, however, might find the story quite intriguing and unnerving. The tale concerns Gilman, a mathematics student, who moves into a room in Arkham once occupied by an old witch named Keziah Mason, who escaped from jail in 1692 and was never seen again. Disappearing with her was her loathsome rat-like familiar called Brown Jenkin. Keziah was rumored to have experimented with "non-Euclidean calculus and quantum physics" in order to find an opening into another dimension. Soon after Gilman moves in, he begins having dreams in which Keziah and Brown Jenkin take him to strange places where time, space, and sound are warped. Matters grow worse and worse, and Gilman is finally found dead in the room, his heart having been eaten by Brown Jenkin.

Curse of the Crimson Altar borrows the idea of a man having dreams in which he is exposed to the horrors of witchcraft. Except for that, the film owes little to its source. There are some small similarities, however, that the casual reader may overlook. For example, in the story the strange angles of Gilman's room have a hypnotic effect on him. In the film, Robert's dreams are caused by drugs and hypnotism. In fact, the prologue of the film reads: "... and drugs of this group can produce the most complex hallucinations, and under their influence it is possible by hypnosis to induce the subject to perform actions he would not normally commit. (Extract from medical journal)." Poor Elder was a victim of Morley's hypnotism as well. In the story, Gilman is pressured to sign the book of Azathoth. In the film, Robert is pressured to sign a large, forbidding book that will give his soul to the dark forces. In the story we read: "He was glad to sink into the vaguely roaring twilight abysses, though the pursuit of that iridescent bubble-congeries and that kaleidoscopic little polyhedron was menacing and irritating." In the film, the dreams begin with a kaleidoscopic effect.

Of course there are many more differences than similarities. For example, Robert Manning is no Gilman. The antique dealer is a straight-shooting fellow uninterested in matters intellectual or occult.

He just wants to find his brother and go to bed with Eve. Also, Lavinia is certainly no Keziah Mason. The hideous crone of the story is replaced by the gorgeous Barbara Steele wearing outlandish headgear featuring ram's horns. Nor do any other characters in the film bear a resemblance to those in the story.

At least the film does not, as many others have, reduce Lovecraft's cosmicism to an anthropomorphic battle between good and evil. The film is that indeed, but this time so is Lovecraft's story, with a little higher mathematics thrown in. It is true that Keziah Mason wants to travel to other dimensions, but it is also clear that she represents traditional dark forces, and the horribly tittering and befanged Brown Jenkin is no extra-terrestrial. No, the evil here is a spawn of old-fashioned Salem witchcraft.

Critique

Curse of the Crimson Altar is little more than an excuse to team Boris Karloff (1887–1969), Christopher Lee (b. 1922), and Barbara Steele (b. 1938). Karloff and Lee had appeared together in Corridors of Blood (1962), a medical melodrama in which Karloff starred and Lee played a minor supporting role. Crimson Altar is Karloff's second (see Die, Monster, Die!) and Lee's, to date, only Lovecraft outing. Of course Boris Karloff came to prominence playing Frankenstein's Monster in 1931, and Christopher Lee essayed the same role in a much different style in Hammer's Curse of Frankenstein (1957). Lee went on to play other roles first played by Karloff in such films as The Mummy (1959) and the Fu Manchu series (1965–1968). It was in Dracula (1958), however, that Lee captured the imagination of the world with his portrayal of the vampire count. Both Karloff and Lee had appeared in dozens of horror films before 1968, and Lee would appear in many more.

British leading lady Barbara Steele (who appeared mainly in Italian films) stunned audiences with her macabre and sensual portrayal of a resurrected witch in Black Sunday (1960). She went on to score in many other chillers.

It was the teaming of these three titans of terror that producers relied on to sell the film. Unfortunately, the film needed something more, such as an engaging script and better direction.

Let's start with the acting. Karloff gets top billing and performs well under trying circumstances. So precarious was his health that producers could not even get insurance on him. Suffering from bronchial trouble and in a wheelchair, Karloff had to sit and perform outdoors in cold, rainy weather; this led to the pneumonia that killed him the next year. Throughout most of the film, he is the red herring we are to believe is behind Peter Manning's disappearance. Indeed, when he talks of witchcraft and such things, his delivery is sinister and suggestive. But we learn at the film's conclusion that he is not the evil one. As Lee walks in flames on the roof, Karloff delivers the following ridiculous lines: "He was mad. For years I suspected he had a split mind." But he also has a nice explanatory monologue among his opening scenes that treats us to Karloff at his 1968 best. When he fires the pistol at Lee near the end of the film, he looks sick, just as sick as he really was.

Christopher Lee is the consummate gentleman as Morley, always polite and always unruffled. In fact, he doesn't even appear perturbed when he must kill his niece or when he faces the flames on the rooftop. Maybe he was possessed by Lavinia all along — an idea that the screenwriters may have lifted from *The Haunted Palace*, based on Lovecraft's *Case of Charles Dexter Ward*, in which a man is possessed by his warlock ancestor.

As for Barbara Steele, Christopher Lee gives probably the best critique of her work in the film: "Barbara had a part that could have been played by any competent actress: she's a damn good actress, and they could have made use of her marvelous qualities."*

Virginia Wetherell, in her first film, is a lovely, capable actress. Mark Eden is okay as the rather uninteresting male lead.

The screenplay is plodding, and director Vernon Sewell (b. 1903) does little to invigorate affairs. Cinematographer John Coquillon was certainly capable of interesting work, as proved by *Witchfinder General* (1968, directed by Michael Reeves), *The Oblong Box* (1969, directed by Gordon Hessler), *The Triple Echo* (1972, directed by Michael Apted) and *Cross of Iron* (1977, directed by Sam Peckinpah). Unfortunately, despite shooting at stately Grimsdyke Hall near Reading, Coquillon is unable to infuse the film with much visual interest.

*Pohle, Robert W., Jr., and Douglas C. Hart. *The Films of Christopher Lee*. Metuchen: N.J.: Scarecrow, 1983.

The opening and closing musical theme sets the right mood; lilting, with just a hint of danger. Otherwise the score veers between unremarkable and inappropriate.

American International apparently had little hope for the film, as it was double-billed with *The Haunted House of Horror* (aka *Horror House*) starring Frankie Avalon. The American pressbook is a skimpy, four-page affair, half devoted to ads featuring the menacing face of Boris Karloff "in his last and most diabolical role." False advertising, to be sure! First of all, this was not Karloff's last film. It was his last British film, but he would appear in four Mexican horror and science fiction films (with his footage shot in the U.S.) before his death. Also, his role is not diabolic. He is on the side of the angels, and his actions save the hero and heroine from the diabolical Christopher Lee.

Another advertising catch-line questions, "Human sacrifice to a blood cult ... or virgin bride to a devil-god?" Audiences are also invited to "Come face to face with naked fear on the altar of evil!" These representations are overblown to say the least.

Unknown to many, both Karloff and Lee were admirerers of Lovecraft. In his 1946 anthology *And Darkness Falls*, Karloff includes "The Thing on the Doorstep." In his introduction to the story, Karloff writes:

> I owe to the courtesy of Mr. William T. Scott, literary editor of *The Providence Journal,* my sudden interest in the works of this writer. Just after my anthology *Tales of Terror* was published, he wrote to me, care of my collaborator, and urged me to include in my next book something from Lovecraft. He then loaned us a copy of that now rare volume *The Outsider and Others,* and with that in hand and *Beyond the Wall of Sleep* also before us, we read many hundreds of pages of stories. We had to reject some because they were too long for a single anthology, others because they were already too well-known, until I decided finally on the narrative which follows.
>
> Whoever wishes to feast on charnel-houses, slathers of primordial evil, cosmic ghouls and demons, terrifying entities that have no name, and lands that exist in neither space nor time, is urged to get these two volumes. Mr. Scott's almost full-page review of the two books (cf. *The Providence Sunday Journal* for December 26, 1943) is a scholarly essay and biography of Lovecraft, and explains why men of *belles lettres* as

distinguished as the late Stephen Vincent Benet, among others, were and are admirerers of Lovecraft, direct literary descendant of Edgar Allan Poe.

In *Boris Karloff's Favorite Horror Stories* (1965) Karloff includes Lovecraft's "The Haunter of the Dark."

Christopher Lee and Michel Parry also edited a couple of horror story anthologies. In *From the Archives of Evil, Number 2*, Lee chooses Lovecraft's "Lurking Fear" and pens the following introduction:

> Although little-known in his lifetime, Howard Phillips Lovecraft has since become recognized as one of the truly great writers of macabre fiction. His influence has been readily acknowledged by such outstanding talented writers as Robert Bloch and August Derleth, who have themselves helped to develop and expand the wonderful mythos of Elder Gods and Great Old Ones which Ech-Pi-El (as Lovecraft signs himself in letters of his in my possession) first conceived. Personally I can think of no better phrase to describe his work than the title of this story. What pictures the word "lurk" conjures up! It suggests Dark Corners and Shadowy People and Ghastly Things ... (I've lurked quite a bit myself from time to time in my professional life!) It is an extremely suggestive word, and its use is typical of Lovecraft, who was undoubtedly one of the most suggestive writers that ever lived. His writing abounds with phrases such as "nameless abominations," phrases which work on your imagination and immediately you begin to envision the most appalling things — who knows, perhaps worse things than Lovecraft ever had in mind when he wrote the story!

Both Karloff and Lee must have been unimpressed with what Tigon and American International did with "The Dreams in the Witch House."
Rating: 2

The Dunwich Horror (1970)
American International, U.S.A.

Produced by James H. Nicholson and Samuel Z. Arkoff. Executive producer, Roger Corman. Directed by Daniel Haller. Screenplay by Curtis Lee Hanson, Henry Rosenbaum, and Ronald Silkosky, based on "The Dunwich Horror" by H.P. Lovecraft. Cinematography by Richard C. Glouner. Edited by Fred Feitshans, Jr., and Christopher Holmes. Art direction by Paul Sylos. Music by Les Baxter. Special effects by Roger George. First assistant director and production manager, Jack Bohrer. Second assistant director, Lew Borzage. Hairdresser, Faith Schmehr. Wardrobe by Dick Bruno. Property master, Ted Berkeley. 90 minutes.

Cast: Sandra Dee (Nancy Walker), Dean Stockwell (Wilbur Whateley), Ed Begley (Dr. Henry Armitage), Sam Jaffe (Old Whateley), Lloyd Bochner (Dr. Cory), Donna Baccala (Elizabeth Hamilton), Joanna Moore Jordan (Lavinia), Talia Coppola (Cora), Barboura Morris (Mrs. Cole), Mike Fox (Dr. Raskin), Jason Wingreen (police chief), Michael Haynes (guard).

Synopsis

Dr. Henry Armitage is a guest lecturer at Miskatonic University on occult subjects, especially those regarding an ancient rare book called *The Necronomicon*, one copy of which is kept in the Miskatonic Library. Wilbur Whateley, a young man from Dunwich, asks Armitage if he might borrow the book for his own occult research. Armitage has written a paper on the Whateley family and on old Oliver Whateley's execution for practicing demonology. Wilbur is Oliver's great-grandson. Reluctant to let such a rare book leave the library, Armitage refuses Wilbur's request.

Wilbur then turns his attention from the book to Armitage's pretty co-ed assistant, Nancy Walker. Wilbur concocts a story of having missed his bus, and Nancy, who is attracted to Wilbur, offers to drive him home. On the way, she is sympathetic when learning that the citizens of Dunwich believe Wilbur and his aged grandfather, Old Whateley, and Wilbur's mother Lavinia (now in a mental hospital) to be sorcerers.

At the Whateley's forbidding farmhouse, Wilbur brews Nancy some strange tea and places her under his influence. She agrees to spend the night in Lavinia's four-poster bed, where she is subjected to dreams of men in goat heads and frenzied revelers trying to induce a sexual orgy.

When Nancy agrees to spend the weekend with Wilbur, her friend Elizabeth Hamilton becomes concerned and goes with Dr. Armitage to visit Dr. Cory, who signed Wilbur's birth certificate. Cory reveals that no record exists of Wilbur's father, but that villagers believe Wilbur is the son of some sort of demon from another dimension. More shocking, Dr. Cory reveals that Lavinia delivered twins that night. What happened to the other child he does not know. Cora, Dr. Cory's nurse, advises Elizabeth to get Nancy out of "Weird Wilbur's" place as soon as possible.

Meanwhile, Wilbur takes Nancy to the top of Sentinel Hill, an eerie promontory near the Whateley house, and shows her the circular altar and stone columns known as the Devil's Hop-yard. He tells her, suggestively, that the Old Ones, beings who once inhabited the earth, used this ceremonial place for fertility rites. He tells her that incantations found in *The Necronomicon* can bring the Old Ones back. What he doesn't tell her is that the human race will be destroyed if he is successful.

Before Nancy and Wilbur return, Elizabeth arrives at the farmhouse and confronts Old Whateley about Nancy's whereabouts. When Old Whateley insists that she leave, she investigates a noise upstairs, opens a door in a secluded part of the house and is destroyed by something inhuman that manifests itself through a surging wind and sharp blasts of sound.

When Wilbur returns, Old Whateley tries to stop Wilbur's work with *The Necronomicon* and dies in a fall down the stairs. Wilbur then steals the book from the library, killing a guard in the process. With Nancy on the altar at the Devil's Hop-yard, Wilbur commences an incantation that causes the creature in the locked room to destroy the Whateley farmhouse and cut a swath of death and destruction on its way to Sentinel Hill.

Armitage arrives at the Devil's Hop-yard with Dr. Cory and a band of townspeople to find Wilbur chanting over an altar where rests a hypnotized and scantily clad Nancy. Though Wilbur has *The Necronomicon*, Dr. Armitage, a student of the occult himself, counters with incantations of his own. Wilbur is unable to control the forces surrounding him, and when the creature arrives, it and Wilbur burst into flames and plummet over the cliff. Dr. Armitage explains to the confused Nancy that Wilbur was only half human and that his father was not of this earth. He then leads the newly pregnant Nancy away from Sentinel Hill.

Adaptation

The premise of both story and film are similar. In the story, the Whateley family of Dunwich, a small town near Arkham, Massachusetts, has long practiced the black arts, including contact with beings from another sphere or dimension. On Candlemass, Wilbur Whateley is born to the unmarried Lavinia Whateley in the family farmhouse several miles from the village. Wilbur, only partly human, wants to study *The Necronomicon* so as to bring the Old Ones back to Earth.

As opposed to the film's rather suave Wilbur, Lovecraft's Wilbur stands about eight feet tall and is very countrified in speech. He possesses few social skills and is most narrow in his interests. While Lovecraft's Wilbur is particularly abominable in appearance below the waist, a fact he can hide with clothing, he is still goat-like, abnormally tall, and socially odd. Dean Stockwell's Wilbur is certainly more attractive in all ways than one could reasonably expect of someone only half human. Dr. Armitage translates well from story to film, as do Old Whateley and Lavinia. Not appearing in the story are Sandra Dee's Nancy, the mandatory threatened female, and her friend Elizabeth.

The first quarter of Lovecraft's story is spent providing a description of Dunwich and of Wilbur's mysterious birth and boyhood. Matters then shift to the university, where Wilbur meets Dr. Armitage and fails in his attempt to borrow *The Necronomicon*. Wilbur returns later to steal the book but is torn to pieces by the library watchdog. The monster from the Whateley farmhouse then breaks loose and moves toward Sentinel Hill, destroying everything in its path.

Dr. Armitage, Professor Rice, and Dr. Morgan (the film's Dr. Cory) go to Sentinel Hill in an effort to stop the creature, which one terrified villager in Lovecraft's story describes as follows:

> Bigger'n a barn ... all made o' squirmin' ropes ... hull thing sort o' shaped like a hen's egg bigger'n anything, with dozens o' legs like hogsheads that haff shut up when they step ... nothin' solid abaout it—all like jelly, an' made o' sep'rit wrigglin' ropes pushed clost together ... great bulgin' eyes all over it ... ten or

twenty maouths or trunks a-stickin' aout all along the sides, big
as stovepipes, an' all a-tossin' an' openin' an' shuttin' ... all grey,
with kinder blue or purple rings ... an' Gawd in heaven — that
haff face on top!

Oh, oh, my Gawd, that haff face — that haff face on top of it
... that face with the red eyes an' crinkly albino hair, an' no
chin, like the Whateleys ... It was a octapus, centipede, spider
sort o' thing, but they was a haff-shaped man's face on top of
it, an' it looked like Wizard Whjateley's, only it was yards an'
yards acrost....

Incredibly, the creature in the film fills the bill quite accurately.

In the story, when the creature is gone, Dr. Armitage explains that
"the thing split up into what it was originally made of, and can never
exist again." Only one part of it was actually matter as humans know
it, and the rest went back to its father in another dimension. The thing
was Wilbur's twin brother, "but it looked more like the father than he
did."

At one point Wizard Whateley scornfully addresses some citizens
of Dunwich, saying, "Ye needn't think the only folks is the folks here-
abaouts," reflecting pride in his family's association with powerful extraterrestrials. In the film, Sam Jaffe utters a similar line with evident
pride and scorn.

In the story, one Dunwich denizen explains the horror as "the
Lord's jedgment fer our iniquities, that no mortal kin ever set aside."
As Joshi notes, for Lovecraft, such an utterance condemns the conven-
tionalism of the speaker. Lovecraft does dabble in religious themes,
however, since Yog-Sothoth, an extraterrestrial being considered a god
by *The Necronomicon*, mates with an earthly virgin and produces a son.
Well, actually two. Wilbur and the Dunwich Horror set out to usher
in the reign of their father's kingdom on earth. This theme is present
but understated in both the story and the film.

In the film, Dunwich citizens are portrayed as rustic, but not as
Lovecraft's inbred simpletons, and no one in the film invokes God as
part of the explanation of events. In fact, the only invoking of God in
the film is the dinner blessing said by Farmer Cole and his wife shortly
before they and their farmhouse are destroyed by the Horror.

In the story, the citizens of Dunwich feel powerless to combat or stop a thing so powerful as the Horror. This fatalism is not shared by the cinematic citizens of Dunwich, who take up torches and rifles to search out the creature. They may as well have been fatalistic, however, as the Horror advances undeterred.

At the story's close, Armitage explains what has happened as best he can to the villagers: "It was — well, it was mostly a kind of force that doesn't belong in our parts of space; a kind of force that acts and grows and shapes itself by other laws than those of our sort of Nature. We have no business calling in such things from outside, and only very wicked people and very wicked cults ever try to."

S.T. Joshi and other Lovecraft scholars ridicule Armitage's words as the "childish and bombastic" utterance of a self-important scholar. In the film, Ed Begley's Armitage is no such buffoon. Though learned, he explains the situation in grave, yet down-to-earth phrases, without moralizing.

Critique

Though *The Dunwich Horror* is flawed as both a Lovecraft adaptation and as a film, it is nevertheless one of the most underrated horror pictures of the 1970s. The opening credits are extraordinary over the shadow artwork of a man and pregnant woman on a journey. The two climb a steep crag that turns out to be the face of Satan, who picks the two up and tosses them down his throat. All of this happens to "Dunwich," Les Baxter's very eerie opening credit music. The main theme repeats with minor variation at various points of the film, always unnerving, always effective. So good was the soundtrack, in fact, that it was released as a record by American International. It remains one of the most evocative horror film soundtracks ever recorded.

Having worked as Roger Corman's art director on *The Haunted Palace* (based on Lovecraft's *Case of Charles Dexter Ward*) and as director under producer Roger Corman on *Die, Monster Die!* (based on Lovecraft's "Colour out of Space"), Daniel Haller returned to direct *The Dunwich Horror*. According to Haller, he (uncredited) and others worked on the screenplay, which was somewhat rushed. Still, the screenplay is well paced, incorporating more of Lovecraft than any other theatrical release with the possible exception of *The Resurrected*.

Leading lady Sandra Dee (b. 1942), who had established herself in such cinematic successes as *Gidget* (1959), *Imitation of Life* (1959), *A Summer Place* (1959), and *Tammy and the Doctor* (1963), was struggling with alcoholism when cast as Nancy in *The Dunwich Horror*. It does not show, however, as she gives a fine performance as a vulnerable young woman engulfed in a web of danger she doesn't understand. Her inner conflict is palpable as she somewhat reluctantly acquiesces to Stockwell's drugs and charm. In one memorable moment, when Stockwell probes to see if she is a virgin, she tries to appear experienced but soon sheepishly admits to only pretending. The pressbook claimed that two sound stages were used during Dee's nude scene, one for the scene and one to lock up stagehands not needed for the scene. In a further effort to keep out "peeping toms," the pressbook reported, police were stationed at stage doors to make sure that no cameras were brought in for secret snapshots. Haller, who had not read the pressbook, denied that any such precautions were taken for Miss Dee since a body double was used and the nudity was so minor as to be inconsequential.

Young veteran actor Dean Stockwell (b. 1935), who had given excellent performances in such films as *The Green Years* (1946), *The Boy with Green Hair* (1948), *Compulsion* (1959), *Sons and Lovers* (1960), and *Long Day's Journey into Night* (1962), gives an excellent performance as Wilbur Whateley. Though he is not the Wilbur conceived by Lovecraft, and though he is too normal to be half-human, he projects sophisticated evil capable of pushing the learned Dr. Armitage to the maximum of his reserves.

Character actor Ed Begley (1901–1970), who had won an Academy Award for his performance in *Sweet Bird of Youth* (1962), is perfect as Dr. Armitage. Though he often played blustery characters, he avoids doing so in *The Dunwich Horror*. His character is sympathetic, strong, and respectable.

Sam Jaffe (1891–1984) had provided memorable performances in such films as *The Scarlet Empress* (1934), *Lost Horizon* (1937), and *Gunga Din* (1939) and had earned an Academy Award nomination for his performance in *The Asphalt Jungle* (1950). He uses his eccentric looks to good advantage as Old Whateley and projects a combination of superiority and fear as he looks down on his simple neighbors while becoming increasingly uncomfortable with his grandson's dangerous plans to prove the villagers wrong one final time. Particularly memorable is the scene in which Jaffe harassed locals in the grocery store, proclaims that "some day yew folks'll hear a child o' Lavinny's a-callin its father's name on the top o' Sentinel Hill."

Canadian leading man Lloyd Bochner (b. 1924) who had worked on television and in occasional films, is well cast as Dr. Cory. With his pipe and serious, relaxed demeanor, he is an exemplary country doctor.

Joanna Moore Jordan turns in a fine performance as mad Lavinia, frothing, screaming, and babbling incoherent mumbo-jumbo in her padded cell. Nice, too, is her death scene as she struggles for life while whippoorwills chirp outside the asylum, waiting to catch her departing soul.

Director Francis Ford Coppola's sister, Talia Coppola (later Talia Shire) (b. 1946), followed up her appearance in *The Wild Racers* (1968) with *The Dunwich Horror*. Though her role is small as Dr. Cory's doomed nurse, she makes the most of her scenes and would later distinguish herself in *The Godfather* (1972) and win Academy Award nominations for performances in *Godfather II* (1974) and *Rocky* (1976).

Though Daniel Haller wishes computer animation had been available in 1970 to produce *The Dunwich Horror*, the actual result is quite satisfying, as nothing quite like it had appeared on screen before. In addition, the abomination with writhing arms and a human face closely approximates that of Lovecraft's story. Some of the most memorable moments in the film consist of the camera moving subjectively from the creature's point of view across the windswept countryside as Les Baxter's musical score bears down. There is one inconsistency, however. In the story, the Horror is invisible and can be seen only briefly when Armitage renders it visible with a device. In the film, the Horror is invisible as it moves cross country, but it inexplicably becomes visible when killing a victim and when destroyed at the end of the film. Speaking of the killings, they are well done. The psychedelic flashes that meet Donna Baccala when she opens the strange door in the farmhouse shock with their power and unexpected nature. In other examples, the camera gives us subjective shots from the Horror's perspective as it looks down from above at the intended victim. Then it moves in and all hell breaks loose.

Location sequences were shot in Mendocino, California, both a pro and a con. According to the pressbook, Haller selected as his Whateley Place a local sprawling, weatherbeaten farmhouse because of its location on a barren hilltop overlooking the Pacific Ocean and because of its foreboding appearance. In fact, all the location sequences are well mounted. On the negative side, Haller used local hippies in Sandra Dee's dream sequences. The dancing, gyrating tribe that ended up on screen is more silly than frightening. Apparently, this motley crew is supposed to represent the Old Ones. If so, it was a poor idea. In the story, Lovecraft mentions Indian tribes that were once up to no good in the region. The charitable viewer may prefer to think that the hippie horde represents them, returned for a bit of cavorting in Dee's subconscious.

In a sense, the making of *The Dunwich Horror* during the time of the hippies was fortuitous since America was worried about cults, the most important being The International Society for Krishna Consciousness. Actually ISKON was not a cult; it was a sect of one of the great world religions, Hinduism. Still, Americans did not understand it and were suspicious. In the film, Nancy is lured into what might be called the cult of Yog-Sothoth, the primary (and possibly only) members being the Whateleys.

The Dunwich Horror is the best Lovecraft theatrical adaptation to date. Most elements combine to produce a film worth repeated viewings. Posters and ads for the film offered interesting and generally apt catch phrases:

> "A few years ago in Dunwich a half-witted girl bore illegitimate twins. One of them was almost human."
>
> "H.P. Lovecraft's terrifying tale of those who explore the unspeakable! Men who invoke its power ... women who invite its shame."
>
> "He invoked the UNSPEAKABLE ... SHE INVITED IT!
>
> "The sound of whippoorwills is the song of death in Dunwich!"
>
> "THE NIGHTS ARE DARKER IN DUNWICH ... and nights are when it happens!"
>
> "People seldom visit Dunwich. The town is ruined, decadent and its annals reek of overt viciousness, murder, incest and deeds of unnameable violence and perversity." — H.P. Lovecraft

The Lovecraft quotation is not a direct quote. In context, the correct quote is: "...the natives are now repellently decadent, having gone far along that path of retrogression so common in many New England backwaters. They have come to form a race by themselves, with all the well-defined mental and physical stigmata of degeneracy and inbreeding. The average of their intelligence is woefully low, whilst their annals reek of overt viciousness and of half-hidden murders, incests, and deeds of almost unnamable violence and perversity."

The pressbook also recommended theaters hype the Lancer paperback *The Dunwich Horror* by H.P. Lovecraft when promoting the film. While the pressbook calls the book a paperback tie-in, it is not one in the usual sense because it nowhere mentions the film on its covers or in its contents.

Rating: 3

Re-Animator (1985)
Empire Pictures, U.S.A.

Directed by Stuart Gordon. Produced by Charles Band, Bruce William Curtis, and Brian Yuzna. Screenplay by Stuart Gordon, William Norris, and Dennis Paoli, based on "Herbert West — Reanimator" by H.P. Lovecraft. Cinematography by Mac Ahlberg. Music by Richard Band. Art direction by Robert Burns. Edited by Lee Percy. 86 minutes.

Cast: Jeffrey Combs (Herbert West), Bruce Abbott (Dan Cain), Barbara Crampton (Megan Halsey), David Gale (Dr. Carl Hill), Robert Sampson (Dean Halsey), and Carolyn Purdy-Gordon (Dr. Harrod).

Synopsis

When young intern Dan Cain is overly zealous in trying to revive an obese heart patient who has died in the emergency room, his superior, Dr. Harrod, reassigns him to the morgue. There he meets young medical genius Herbert West, who has just arrived at Miskatonic Medical School after studying (with some unfortunate results) in Switzerland. Dr. Carl Hill, Miskatonic's eminent brain surgeon and fund-raiser, takes an immediate dislike to West when the young man remarks that Hill's methods are outdated. West, who researches the field of death, claims that the brain can survive longer after being deprived of oxygen than Hill believes. Allen Halsey, medical school dean, tries to keep the peace. Meanwhile, Dan Cain is dating and having sex with Megan Halsey, the dean's lovely daughter.

Dan reluctantly allows Herbert West to rent a room in his house after West surprises Dan and Megan in a compromising position. Megan soon discovers Dan's cat missing and finds it frozen in West's refrigerator. West claims unconvincingly that the cat suffocated by accident. Later, Dan hears a struggle in the basement and finds the recently deceased cat clawing the hell out of West. Dan throws the cat against a wall, breaking its back and killing it. When West claims that he reanimated the cat with a reagent he discovered, Dan assumes that the cat had never really died in the first place. However, Dan becomes a believer when West reanimates the broken-backed cat before his eyes.

West and Cain decide to experiment on corpses in the morgue. Unfortunately, the first specimen they reanimate goes on a mindless rampage and murders Dean Halsey. West and Cain reanimate Halsey, only to see him turn into a blood-drooling maniac. Halsey is placed in an asylum by Dr. Hill, who has amorous designs on Megan himself. Hill finds out that West is reanimating corpses and hypnotizes West in a successful attempt to steal the reagent formula. While Hill is examining West's notes, West attacks from behind and cuts off Hill's head with a shovel. West then uses a paper spike to place Hill's head upright in a pan, and reanimates Hill's head and trunk. Hill's headless body knocks West unconscious and leaves with the head and reanimation serum. Hill's various parts then induce the mad Dean Halsey to lay out his unconscious daughter on a morgue table. Hill's body places his head next to Megan's face, and the leering head's tongue begins to explore Megan's face and ear. West arrives and confronts headless Hill and his severed head. West is overcome by reanimated intestines when drooling, naked corpses reanimated by Hill leap from body bags and attack. Megan is killed by one of the reanimated corpses, and Dan arrives in time to inject her with the reagent.

Adaptation

When *Re-Animator* was released, people familiar with Lovecraft's classic tales dismissed the film as a cynical use of the author's name to trick his fans and appeal to a target audience of jaded teenagers. After all, blood-saturated stills from the film appeared on the covers of gore-oriented film magazines everywhere. But this time the cynics were wrong. In fact, Lovecraft wrote the six parts of "Herbert West — Reanimator" at the request of a weird-fiction magazine called *Home Brew*. Lovecraft had no respect for the publication and lowered his usual standards for the money. The result was a black comedy in which Lovecraft gave the magazine's audience what he thought it demanded: mindless horror and gore for its own sake. Therefore, the film emerges as a remarkably good adaptation.

Similarities between story and film abound. In the story, for example, Herbert West and the narrator are third year students at Miskatonic University Medical School in Arkham. West experiments with cats and other animals in an effort to reanimate the dead, but he notices that the revived creatures exhibit violent behavior. West believes that "the psychic or intellectual life might be impaired by the slight deterioration of sensitive brain-cells which even a short period of death would be apt to cause." This would explain the violence of his reanimated subjects. Enthralled by West's experiments, the narrator becomes his willing assistant. The film adapts all of this.

Dr. Halsey, the medical school dean, disapproves of West's work and bars him from the university. In the film, it is the narrator who is banned. In the story, West and the narrator move to a farmhouse and continue their experiments. While this move does not occur in the film, the story does have West and the narrator obtaining subjects from the morgue. In both story and film, West reanimates Dr. Halsey, who becomes a monster incarcerated in an asylum, "where it beats its head against the wall of a padded cell." In the story, West and the narrator enlist as medical men in World War I in order to acquire fresh bodies. This results in the two scholars experimenting on a soldier recently killed in a plane crash. West decapitates the corpse and reanimates both head and body, but not with the awful results depicted in the film. In the last section of Lovecraft's work, West and the narrator decapitate the corpse of a physician familiar with their work "so that the possibilities of quasi-intelligent life in the trunk might be investigated.... [West] used to make shuddering conjectures about the possible actions of a headless physician with the power of reanimating the dead." The resulting abomination is "a menacing military figure who talked without moving his lips and whose voice seemed almost ventriloquially connected with an immense black case he carried. His expressionless face was handsome to the point of radiant beauty, but had shocked the superintendent when the hall light fell on it — for it was a wax face with eyes of painted glass." This is how Dr. Hill gets about after his cinematic resurrection. Though the film goes over the top in ways foreign to the story, the story contains some moments of horror that rival anything in the film. On the whole, *Re-Animator* is a good adaptation of Lovecraft's story in terms of both plot and tone.

Popular culture at the time accounts for the film being so un-Lovecraftian in its reliance on gore and sex. Since the 1970s, horror films had been aiming for a jaded male teenage audience. The more producers piled horror upon horror, the more the target audience required. The incidence of both graphic and suggested sex had grown precipitously throughout this time period as well. In fact, a new type of film fan know as the "gorehound" evolved. Without a doubt, the gorehound could track down a satisfying amount of blood and gore in *Re-Animator.*

So, were horror films improved as a result of the gorehound phenomenon? Probably not, at least for viewers who were used to shock theater and the horror films of the fifties and sixties. Gorehound films usually sacrifice subtlety and imagination for human interest. The characters become dehumanized death vehicles for the bloody stalker or psycho killer. Still, within this subgenre there are some very good films, proving that broad generalizations are rarely accurate.

Critique

Director Stuart Gordon (b. 1947) broke in as an artistic director in a Chicago theater with a company called Organic Theater. Gordon wanted to shoot a horror film with the theater troupe and looked about for a vehicle. A friend suggested "Herbert West — Reanimator." Though Gordon had read and enjoyed Lovecraft, he had never heard of that particular story. He soon found it in an out-of-print book and adopted it as his project. The theater's board of directors did not believe that the troupe's first film should be a horror film, so Gordon took a leave of absence from the theater, received funding from producer Brian

Yuzna (b. 1949), and went to work with a budget of about $800,000. The film was shot in 18 days. In *Re-Animator*, Gordon gets good work from his cast and keeps the film fast paced.

In approaching his first film, director Gordon knew little about the craft of cinema but learned on the job from Swedish director and cinematographer Mac Ahlberg (b. 1931). Ahlberg had commanded the camera in such previous horror films as *Nocturna* (1978), *Hell Night* (1981), *Parasite* (1982), and *Ghoulies* (1985). In *Re-Animator*, Ahlberg makes good use of closeups, especially those of actor David Gale, and he allows the camera to gorge on blood and guts to achieve the desired effect.

Richard Band's opening music, played over pages from *Gray's Anatomy*, is a funny disco remix of Bernard Hermann's *Psycho* theme. Another plus is Lee Percy's editing, as when he cuts quickly from the reanimated broken-backed cat, providing us with just an appalling peek. The dialogue is humorous and pithy. For example, note the following exchange between West and Dan Cain:

> WEST: I had to kill him [Dr. Hill].
> DAN: Dead?
> WEST: Not anymore.
> DAN: Oh, Herbert, this has got to stop!

And when disgusted by the antics of Dr. Hill's severed head, West tells the head to "get a job in a sideshow."

The cast is headed by Jeffrey Combs, who is a perfect Herbert West, described by Lovecraft as a "small, slender spectacled youth with delicate features." Combs came to the film with stage experience in both Shakespeare and light comedy. Anthony Band, the casting director for *Re-Animator*, approached Combs in connection with a play he was also casting and recommended that Combs see "some friends of mine" about a role in an upcoming picture. That film was *Re-Animator*. Combs considered the script very bloody, but also funny. According to Combs, director Gordon did not consider the film funny at all; he considered it a straight horror film. Doubting that the film would work if played completely straight, Combs took a page from Vincent Price and played the role fairly straight but with tongue in cheek — and the result could not have been better.

Some funny things in the film were not scripted. According to Combs, he was supposed to set Dr. Hill's severed head upright in a pan, but he could not get the head to stand upright. So he "did the threes." Explained Combs, "You know. I took the head assuming it was going to stand up and it slips, so I pick it up again and it slips, too. So I go to the letter stand and boom, bop [he impales the head], it worked. Thank goodness the prop master had it out for me to use."* Combs would go on to star in several more Lovecraft films and distinguish himself in television's *Star Trek: Deep Space Nine* (1996–).

The rest of the cast performs admirably, even the reanimated mad-men who provide much of the film's most grotesque action. David Gale is appropriately absurd as the hypnotic Dr. Hill, and Robert Sampson does a good transformation from bumbling dean to slobbering maniac.

Posters for the film featured mad Herbert West in the laboratory with a fuming test tube in his hand and the head of Dr. Hill on the table before him. Capturing the mood of the film, the catch line reads: "Herbert West has a good head on his shoulders ... and another one on his desk." The poster also describes the film as "H.P. Lovecraft's Classic Tale of Horror ... It Will Scare You to Pieces."

Perhaps surprisingly, *Re-Animator* won first prize at the Paris Festival of Fantasy, Science Fiction, and Horror and a special prize at the Cannes Film Festival. Pocket Books issued a paperback tie-in by Jeff Rovin based on the screenplay. The book cover features a slightly altered catch line: "Herbert West has a very good head on his shoulders ... and another in a dish on his desk." On the book cover, West prepares to inject the head of Dr. Hill, which lies in a dish, as the head-less body of Hill sneaks up from behind. Also available at the time of the film's release was a comic book series based on Herbert West's exploits.

Rating: 3

---

*All Combs references: Migliore, Andrew and John Strysik. *The Lurker in the Lobby: A Guide to the Cinema of H.P. Lovecraft.* Seattle: Pagan Publishing, 2000.

From Beyond (1986)

Empire Pictures, U.S.A.

Directed by Stuart Gordon. Produced by Charles Band, Bruce William Curtis, and Brian Yuzna. Screenplay by Stuart Gordon, Dennis Paoli, and Brian Yuzna, based on the story by H.P. Lovecraft. Cinematography by Mac Ahlberg; Music by Richard Band. 85 minutes.

Cast: Jeffrey Combs (Crawford Tillinghast), Barbara Crampton (Dr. Katherine McMichaels), Ken Foree (Leroy "Bubba" Brown), Ted Sorel (Dr. Edward Pretorius), Carolyn Purdy-Gordon (Dr. Bloch), Bunny Summers (neighbor lady).

Synopsis

Strange experiments are progressing in an attic laboratory at 666 Benevolent Street. Crawford Tillinghast uses a "resonator," four large tuning forks atop a glowing globe, to stimulate his own pineal gland. This pineal stimulation allows Tillinghast to see strange eel-like creatures circling the forks in midair. Bowing to curiosity, Tillinghast steps forward for a better look, but a creature senses his movement and ferociously bites his cheek. Crawford shuts off the machine and races downstairs to tell his collaborator, Dr. Pretorius. Even more curious than Tillinghast, Pretorius turns the machine up nearly full blast, moans as his pineal gland is stimulated, and announces to Tillinghast that "something's coming." Indeed something does, blowing out the windows of the attic and eating Pretorius' head. Tillinghast destroys the machine and runs for his life, after which he is charged with Pretorius' murder and confined to a mental asylum when nobody accepts his story.

Later, beautiful psychiatrist Katherine McMichaels believes Tillinghast's story and arranges to have him released in her care if he will repair the machine and continue the experiments in her presence. Terrified, Tillinghast reluctantly agrees. The two are joined in the lab by Police Sergeant Leroy "Bubba" Brown.

When the machine is up and running, the trio are shocked to see the naked Dr. Pretorius apparently restored to life in the resonator's red glow. The apparition praises its new existence and invites the trio to join it. But Tillinghast touches Pretorius, revealing the skin to be a putrid form of synthetic putty. "That will be quite enough of that,"

Tillinghast responds, turning off the machine. Katherine talks the men into taking a nap, after which she becomes sexually aroused just contemplating the resonator.

McMichaels turns on the machine and turns into a nymphomaniac. Then Pretorius returns and transforms into a giant worm. A battle ensues in the basement, and Bubba cuts the electricity just as the worm is sucking in Tillinghast, rendering him bald and unconscious.

Pretorius starts the resonator "from beyond," and, caught in the vibrations, Tillinghast's pineal gland grows, snake-like, out of his forehead. Pretorius then lays one of the grossest "kisses" in film history on McMichaels. McMichaels incapacitates the machine and takes Tillinghast to the hospital, after which she herself is incarcerated by the straightlaced Nurse Bloch. Tillinghast then runs amuck, sucks the brains out of Dr. Bloch and returns with McMichaels to the lab where he attempts to suck out her brains when she tries to blow up the resonator. McMichaels escapes an unpleasant fate by biting off Tillinghast's writhing pineal gland, after which Tillinghast and the apparition of Pretorius battle to their deaths in a welter of cosmic cellular chaos.

The windows explode and McMichaels is blasted through the attic window. Later, reduced to a laughing madwoman, she is a permanent patient in the asylum where she once worked.

Adaptation

Lovecraft apparently found the inspiration for "From Beyond" in Hugh Elliot's book *Modern Science and Materialism* (1919), in which the author writes, "Men have five or six senses only.... Now, supposing that we happened to have a thousand senses instead of five, it is clear that our conception of the Universe would be extremely different from what it now is." In a similar vein, Lovecraft's Tillinghast wonders,

> What do we know ... of the world and the universe about us? Our means of receiving impressions are absurdly few, and our notions of surrounding objects infinitely narrow. We see things only as we are constructed to see them, and can gain no idea of their absolute nature. With five feeble senses we pretend to comprehend the boundlessly complex cosmos, yet other beings with a wider, stronger, or different range of senses might not

only see very differently the things we see, but might see and study whole worlds of matter, energy, and life which lie close at hand yet can never be detected with the senses we have.

The opening scenes of "From Beyond" constitute a reasonably faithful adaptation of Lovecraft's seven-and-a-half-page page story. In the story, scientist and philosopher Crawford Tillinghast lures the narrator to his laboratory for pineal gland experiments that allow people to see into another dimension. The foundation of Tillinghast's work is Descartes' theory that the pineal gland "is the great sense-organ of organs.... It is like sight in the end, and transmits visual pictures to the brain. If you are normal, that is the way you ought to get most of it.... I mean get most of the evidence from beyond." Tillinghast's servants have already disappeared as a result of being present when the machine was tested, and Tillinghast desires to sacrifice the narrator next. In the film, however, Tillinghast harbors no evil intent. He is simply the assistant of Dr. Pretorius (undoubtedly named after the character played by Ernest Thesiger in James Whale's 1935 classic, *The Bride of Frankenstein*).

The film faithfully portrays the experiment Lovecraft describes. For example, when the "detestable electrical machine," which makes strange music and a "sickly, sinister, violet luminosity," is activated, Tillinghast and the narrator see "great jellyish monstrosities." In both story and film, Tillinghast warns everyone to "keep still," for the entities from beyond can see them just as they can see the entities.

In the story, a creature from beyond attacks the narrator, who fires his pistol into the machine, ending the experiment and causing Tillinghast's death by apoplexy. In the film, Dr. Pretorius, who does not exist in the story, rushes upstairs and goes hog-wild with desire for new experiences. The creature that never gets at Lovecraft's narrator bites off Pretorius' head. As Tillinghast says of Pretorius, "The five senses weren't enough for him. He wanted more."

Lovecraft's story having been used up in the film's opening sequences, the rest of the film works from a screenplay that owes little to the author and injects copious amounts of gore, violence, sex, and some humor.

In both story and film, Benevolent Street is the ironic address where Tillinghast builds and tests an electrical machine designed to stimulate the pineal gland. The screenwriters supply the numerical 666, the Bible's number symbolic of the Great Beast.

In 1920, Lovecraft told Duane Rimel in a letter that "From Beyond" was "rejected by all paying magazines." The author apparently agreed with the editors' decision, opining that the story would make "excellent shelf paper, but little else."

Critique

With *From Beyond,* director Stuart Gordon wanted to avoid the label of comic horror attributed by critics and audiences to *Re-Animator.* Though there are a few nice comic touches as mentioned above, he largely succeeds.

Jeffrey Combs is excellent as Crawford Tilllinghast, a role quite different from that of Herbert West. Where Combs' West was arrogant and fearless, his Tillinghast is careful and frightened. Is it sexist to say that Barbara Crampton is almost too young and beautiful to be entirely believable as the experimental psychiatrist? Be that as it may, she is easy on the eyes and generates some true pathos as she loses control of herself and degenerates into a leather-clad sensualist. Speaking of sexism, the screenplay acknowledges its existence when Leroy "Bubba" Brown, upon first meeting Dr. McMichaels and Tillinghast, automatically assumes that the male is the professional and the female the patient.

The makeup crew succeeds admirably. Applying Combs' writhing pineal gland took about two hours. First the crew glued a bald cap to the actor's head and then applied a tight-fitting headband with a socket in the center. Wires were fed through four holes in the socket to the back where they were connected to a joy stick. The gland would move in whatever direction the joy stick dictated. Said Combs with a laugh, "It looked like a red asparagus spear, but I always thought it looked like a dog dick." Of course, all the gooey putrid ooze we come to associate with Gordon's Lovecraft pictures continues to work here as well. The small element of the audience looking for a faithful Lovecraft adaptation left theaters angry and disappointed. The film did well at the box office, however, because a generation of young horror movie fans accustomed to gratuitous gore and sex were well pleased with the result.

Posters and ads for the film carried the chilling catch-line

"Humans are such easy prey," uttered by Dr. Pretorius at a crucial point in the film.

Rating: 2½

The Curse (1987)
Trans World Entertainment, U.S.A. and Italy

Directed by David Keith. Produced by Ovidio G. Assonitis. Assistant producer, Louis (Lucio) Fulci. Screenplay by David Chaskin, based on "The Colour Out of Space" by H.P. Lovecraft. Cinematography by Robert D. Forges. Edited by Claude Cutry. Music by Frank Micalizzi. Production designed by Frank Vanorio. Executive producers, Moshe Diamant and Ovidio G. Assonitis. Makeup by Frank Russell. Special effects by Paul Richmond, Burt Spiegell, Steve Massey, and Al Simon. 92 minutes.

Cast: Wil Wheaton (Zach), Claude Akins (Nathan Crane), Malcom Danare (Cyrus Crane), Cooper Huckabee (Dr. Alan Forbes), John Schneider (Carl Willis), Amy Wheaton (Alice), Steve Carlisle (Charley Davidson), Kathleen Jordon Gregory (Frances), Hope North (Esther Forbes), Steve Davis (Mike).

Synopsis

Religious fundamentalist Nathan Crane has married the widow Frances and taken in her three children, Zach, Cyrus, and Alice. With growing bitterness, Nathan struggles to keep his Tennessee farm solvent. Always ready to buy the farmland because of insider information regarding a proposed water reservoir is real estate tycoon Charley Davidson.

One night a meteorite lands on the Crane property. Nathan awakens to find his frustrated wife stealing out of the farmhand's cottage. Young Zach also sees the meteorite and reports it to his neighbor, Dr. Alan Forbes. Dr. Forbes wants to report the meteorite to the Environmental Protection Agency, but Nathan convinces him to study the meteorite himself. The thing quickly shrinks, however, leading Dr. Forbes to conclude that it was just a space pebble filled with escaping carbon dioxide.

The apples and tomatoes that spring from the ground are large and beautiful on the outside, but the Cranes discover them worm-ridden and putrid on the inside. The meteorite contained an alien substance or life form that contaminates the farmland and initiates the mental and physical deterioration of the Crane family. Only Zach realizes what is happening and refuses to drink the water and eat the farm produce. He also protects his little sister, Alice. First the farm animals go mad, followed by Frances, Cyrus, and Nathan. Charley and Esther Forbes are killed while visiting the farm, and the farmhouse itself finally self-destructs, consuming Nathan, Frances, and Cyrus. Zach and Alice are rescued by Dr. Forbes, who realized the truth after having the water tested.

Adaptation

The Curse is a better adaptation of Lovecraft's "The Colour Out of Space" than is its predecessor, *Die, Monster, Die!* (1965). Set and filmed on location in Tellico Plains, Tennessee, the film captures the rural atmosphere missing in the 1965 production set in an English mansion. Tellico Plains isn't Lovecraft's New England, but it is an improvement. The storyline too is more faithful to Lovecraft. In Lovecraft's story, the farm family goes mad one by one, the vegetation is strangely affected, animal life undergoes disturbing changes, and a good-hearted neighbor tries to help. The same elements are in the film.

Also at work in the film is Lovecraft's distrust of religion. Praying without ceasing, Nathan Crane (Nahum in the story) represents a throwback to America's Puritan roots. But his praying has no effect on "the real world." His puritanism drives his wife to adultery, and his prayers to God produce no positive results. There is either no God (as Lovecraft would have it), or God does not answer (as deists would have it). Of course, there is a third possibility, one that neither Lovecraft nor deists would consider. Perhaps Nathan's prayers are unsuccessful simply because Nathan is devout to a fault. Perhaps if he had been a more well-rounded individual, God would have listened. I will address this aspect again in the Critique section on this film.

Let's look at two other similarities between story and film. In the story, Lovecraft describes the trees moving when there is no wind: "The trees budded prematurely around Nahum's, and at night they swayed ominously in the wind. Nahum's second son Thaddeus, a lad of fifteen, swore that they swayed also when there was no wind; but even the gossips would not credit this." A similar phenomenon occurs in the film.

Another similarity between story and film is the final disintegration of Frances Hayes. In the story she devolves into something so loathsome that the narrator avoids a fleshed-out description. In the film, Frances devolves into something quite loathsome, sitting and expiring in a pool of her own contaminated goo. In terms of adaptation, this scene falls short of Lovecraft's handling but is an improvement over the deterioration of Letitia Whitley in *Die, Monster, Die!*

Some critics have wondered why the farmhouse finally self-destructs. It is because without this event, Lovecraft's idea of an alien life form is absent from the film. Though the meteorite changes the molecular composition of the water and has other natural effects, only an alien presence could bring down the house, so to speak. This places *The Curse* in the tradition of other films in which unknown powers destroy houses or whatever else they please. But why does the alien presence bring down the farmhouse? This is unfortunately left unclear. Regardless, humanity's religions pale before such power in Lovecraft's godless universe. Perhaps we are simply unable to understand because of the completely alien nature of the causes we confront.

Critique

The Curse begins with police arriving in a nice city neighborhood or suburb to remove a disfigured man who raves of something being in the water. Is the man telling the truth? What is in the water, if anything? Why is his face disfigured? The body of the film itself is an account of what happened before the prologue, which is never revisited. Therefore, as the film ends, we are left with a warning of unresolved biological and psychological horror.

Much of the film's tension is provided by the effect of Nathan Crane's religious fundamentalism on the members of his family. It seems that Nathan, the natural father of Cyrus, took in Frances and her two children when they needed someone most. But God has not been very good to Nathan as he struggles to keep the family farm afloat. Claude Akins is well-cast as Nathan; his rigidity alienates the rest of the family with the exception of Cyrus, his irritating slob of a natural son. In an early scene, Cyrus plays a practical joke that lands Zach in a pile of dung. When the boys fight, frustrated Nathan breaks them up and quotes Romans 12:10—"Be kindly affectioned one to another with brotherly love." But when Zach utters a curse word, Nathan ironically shows his kindly affection by slapping Zach hard across the face, an act to which he resorts every time Zach acts against his wishes.

When Nathan rejects poor Frances' bedtime sexual advances, she leaves the house late at night and allows herself to be seduced by the farmhand. The meteorite coming at an inopportune time awakens Nathan, allowing him to discover her infidelity. He considers the deterioration of his family and farm as God's punishment for Frances' sin.

The Curse conforms with other horror films of the late 1980s in considering religion a social threat (e.g. *The Blob*, 1988) or as irrelevant, well-meaning foolishness (e.g. *Lady in White*, 1988) and in challenging traditional notions of family values (e.g. *The Stepfather*, 1987, and *Parents*, 1988). The idea that religion is metaphysically separate from reality is pure Lovecraft, and Lovecraft never had much good to say about families either. *The Curse* is an example of a film adaptation of a literary work out of sync with its time being adapted when it was culturally in sync. In many ways, the 1980s and beyond are ready for Lovecraft in ways earlier decades never were.

Rating: 2½

The Unnamable (1988)
Yankee Classic Pictures, U.S.A.

Directed by Jean-Paul Ouellette. Screenplay by Jean-Paul Ouellette, based on "The Unnamable" by H.P. Lovecraft. Produced by Jean-Paul Ouellette, Dean Ramser, and Paul White. Music by David Bergeaud. Cinematography by Tom Fraser. Edited by Paul White. Special makeup effects by R. Christopher Biggs. Executive producer, Paul White. 87 minutes.

Cast: Charles King (Howard Damon), Mark Kinsey Stephenson (Randolph Carter), Alexandra Durrell (Tanya Heller), Laura Albert (Wendy Barnes), Eben Ham (Bruce Weeks), Blane Wheatley (John

Babcock), Mark Parra (Joel Manton), Delbert Spain (Joshua Winthrop), Colin Cox (Mr. Craft), Katrin Alexandre (Alyda Winthrop, the Creature).

Synopsis

In the eighteenth century, Joshua Winthrop hides a secret in his attic. According to a legend attributed to colonial witch-hunter Cotton Mather, the thing in the attic is Winthrop's howling, deformed daughter, whose image is said to linger in the glass of an attic window.

The film then cuts to a graveyard in the present time where student Randolph Carter tells Mather's legend to fellow Miskatonic University students Joel Manton and Howard Damon. An argument soon develops between scientific realist Manton and metaphysician and folklorist Carter as to whether or not such legends could be true. Damon believes that the legend can easily be proven or disproven simply by entering the house and observing what is there. Fearing that evil entities exist in some New England houses, Carter wants no part of such an experiment. When Carter points out that the house in question sits next to the graveyard within sight of the students, Manton decides to conduct his investigation alone. His friends return to the university.

Whatever lurks in the house slaughters Manton, and when his friends note his absence, Carter agrees to accompany Damon to the house after consulting some occult books in the Miskatonic Library's special collection.

At the same time, two frat boys talk a couple of girls into spending the night in the accursed house as practice for an upcoming sorority initiation. When all concerned wind up in the house at night, more bloody murders occur.

Carter discovers a copy of the dreaded *Necronomicon* in Winthrop's decaying library and learns that the old man had planted mystical trees in the yard, hoping that the wood spirits would keep his daughter Alyda imprisoned in the house. Carter descends into Winthrop's tomb with *The Necronomicon* in an effort to stop the horror. The tree spirit comes to the rescue: branches from the giant tree by the tomb pull the creature Alyda through the window and down into the tomb, leaving Carter, Damon, and the girl Tanya as survivors.

Adaptation

Scholars consider "The Unnamable" one of the Lovecraft's lesser efforts. What intrigues them most about the story is its theoretical defense of weird fiction as a literary genre, an element completely ignored by the film. Both story and film begin in a graveyard setting. Lovecraft writes:

> We were sitting on a dilapidated seventeenth-century tomb in the late afternoon of an autumn day at the old burying-ground in Arkham, and speculating about the unnamable. Looking toward the giant willow in the centre of the cemetery, whose trunk has nearly engulfed an ancient, illegible slab, I had made a fantastic remark about the spectral and unmentionable nourishment which the colossal roots must be sucking in from that hoary, charnel earth; ...

The first person narrator is weird fiction author Randolph Carter. His friend, Joel Manton, a high school principal, objects to Carter's talk of the unnamable and unmentionable, claiming that "we know things ... only through our five senses or our religious institutions." He calls Carter's talk "a very puerile device" quite in keeping with his friend's lowly standing as an author. The film adapts the graveyard setting and the argument between Carter and Manton about the reality of the supernatural.

In the story, Carter defends his weird fiction with reference to a story he had written called "The Attic Window," arguing that "the mind can find its greatest pleasure in escape from the daily treadmill, and in original and dramatic re-combinations of images usually thrown by habit and fatigue into the hackneyed patterns of actual existence." Carter says that his story "The Attic Window" concerns a legend related by Cotton Mather in *Magnalia Christi Americana*. Therein, Mather reports of a bitter, childless old man who keeps something terrible locked in the attic of his house. The old man was buried behind the house in 1710. In an ancestral diary, Carter discovered the location of the house and found that some creature reputedly attacked people in the vicinity. The creature had attacked one of Carter's ancestors, "on a dark valley road, leaving him with marks of horns on his chest and of ape-like claws on his back; and when they looked for prints in the trampled dust they found the mixed marks of split hooves and vaguely anthropoid paws."

Carter suggests that Manton himself half believes "in the impressions left by old faces on the windows through which they had gazed all their lives," and such is said to have been the case in the attic of the old house. Carter goes on to relate the story of a boy who went screaming mad after visiting the attic in 1793. The house in question, Carter points out, stands next the very graveyard where they sit. In fact, Carter had visited the place on one occasion, saw an image in the window, and removed odd bones from the premises. Upon the legends and upon his own experience, Carter had fashioned the story he subsequently sold to *Whispers* magazine.

In the film, Carter and Manton are university students, and Carter has never visited the house personally. Even so, many elements from Lovecraft's story are worked into the film's opening minutes. Carter, for example, is a writer of weird fiction, which Manton calls trash. As in the story, Carter tells of a family diary wherein he learned of a young man going mad upon visiting the house. As in the story, a bat buzzes the young men as they sit in the graveyard. Lovecraft's story ends when the young men are attacked in the graveyard by some unnamable creature, a fact that quickly turns Manton into a believer. In the film, Manton goes to the house to investigate, his friends leave the graveyard, and the film goes on from there. In other words, Lovecraft supplies the film's general premise and main character, which serve as the foundation of an otherwise very un-Lovecraftian film. The unnamable creature does attack Carter and his friends, but the attacks occur in the house, not outside in the graveyard. In addition, Lovecraft gives us little description of the creature, whereas, during its final minutes, the film reveals the creature in all its beastliness.

Though *The Necronomicon* and a fleeting mention of Cthulhu are certainly Lovecraftian elements found in the film, they play no role in Lovecraft's "The Unnamable."

Critique

This film starts with promise and ends with a bang, but plods through familiar genre situations in between. The true-to-Lovecraft graveyard setting and early dialogue provide an eerie tone, partly due to Mark Kinsey Stephenson's engaging and believable characterization of Randolph Carter. Then matters head downhill with the introduction of several horny boys, a horny girl, and a "nice" girl who enter the house as practice for a sorority initiation. Then the horny boys and horny girl are killed by the creature. Between killings there is much corridor walking and sex talk, all of which gets very old very quickly. Director Roger Corman had worn out corridor walking as a source of suspense as early as the late sixties, and a plethora of repetitive films featuring killers stalking horny teenagers (e.g. four sequels spawned by *Halloween* (1978–1989), eight sequels spawned by *Friday the 13th* (1980–1989), *Happy Birthday to Me* (1980), *My Bloody Valentine* (1981), and countless others) were definitely wearing out their welcome. In most of these films, the killer isolates a teenager, kills him or her, and continues stalking the others, most of whom are too stupid or too preoccupied with sex to get the hell out of danger. In most of these films, too, there is a nice, sexually inactive girl who survives. These elements are trotted out yet again in *The Unnamable*, completely to the film's detriment.

The film's finale is a shocker, thanks largely to Katrin Alexandre's portrayal of Alyda, the creature. Stomping on cloven hooves through a window, she is a ferocious apparition nearly unequalled in the horror cinema. Her clutching claws are fearsome. Her horned head and her legs below the knees are covered with long white hair. Fangs glisten in her howling mouth. On her scaly back are what appear to be closed bat wings. Her bat-like ears are pointed. One must see this creature to understand the full impact of Alexandre's performance and R. Christopher Biggs' awesome makeup. Yet, despite the creature's vicious power and obvious malevolence, Alexandre outstandingly manages to convey a touch of vulnerability through the makeup.

Director Ouellette does tip his hat to a few other Lovecraft-inspired films. For example, in the opening sequence, the father coaxes the creature back into the attic room as the camera records the event from the creature's perspective. A similar approach is used in the opening sequence of David Greene's *The Shuttered Room*. Also in the opening sequence, the creature attacks her father (who is a spitting image of John Carradine in *Terror in the Wax Museum*). As in Daniel Haller's *Dunwich Horror*, the creature's approach is punctuated by loud heartbeats. Director Ouellette may also have been influenced a bit by Lovecraft's short story "The Tree," the ending of which more resembles the film's ending than does that of "The Unnamable." This, however, may be a reach.

One final point might be made about the film's teen sexuality. Lovecraft, who had little if any sexual inclination, wrote in a letter to R. Kleiner, E.H. Cole, and F.B. Long that "permissiveness in fornication would logically lead to demands for similar liberty in sodomy, incest, and bestiality. These would be justified as 'honest and progressive.'" So in Lovecraft's view, free sex would lead to bad results. Since the film's sexually active teens certainly come to a bad end, perhaps we can in a sense conclude that they should have heeded Lovecraft's warning (had they known of it).

Rating: 1½

Bride of Re-Animator (1991)
Wild Street, U.S.A.

Directed by Brian Yuzna. Produced by Brian Yuzna and Paul White; Screenplay by Rick Fry, Woody Keith, and Brian Yuzna, based on "Herbert West — Reanimator" by H.P. Lovecraft. Music by Richard Band. Cinematography by Rick Fichter. Special makeup and visual effects by Screaming Mad George, K.N.B. EFX Group, Magical Media Industries, Anthony Doublin, and David Allen. 99 minutes.

Cast: Jeffrey Combs (Herbert West), Bruce Abbott (Dan Cain), Claude Earl Jones (Lt. Leslie Chapham), Fabiana Udenio (Francesca Danelli), David Gale (Dr. Carl Hill), Kathleen Kinmont (Gloria the Bride).

Synopsis

Eight months after the Miskatonic Massacre represented by the finale of *Re-Animator* (1985), Herbert West and Dan Cain serve as medics in a Peruvian civil war. When their camp is overrun by the enemy, the doctors' continued medical experiments in life and death are interrupted.

The doctors resume residency in Arkham at Miskatonic University, where Police Detective Leslie Chapham, whose wife was left a walking, blubbering corpse at the end of *Re-Animator*, is still investigating the case. In the course of his work, he finds and returns the head of Dr. Hill, West's mortal enemy, to Dr. William Graves, the hospital's pathologist. Chapham is concerned to learn that body parts are disappearing right and left from hospital storage.

Later, West discovers Dr. Hill's head in hospital storage and remarks, "Look at you now. You're nothing but a dead head." Dr. Graves, however, discovers West's reagent in storage and reanimates both a dead bat and Dr. Hill's head. Eventually he sews the bat's wings onto Hill's head, creating an odd creature that flies and talks.

Meanwhile, West and Cain work at constructing a woman out of body parts, including the heart of Cain's departed sweetheart, Meg. In the basement lab, Cain injects Gloria, the newly constructed "Bride," with the reagent, bringing her to life. When it becomes clear that the Bride is nothing like Meg, Cain rejects her. Distraught by rejection, the Bride rips out Meg's heart and hands it to Cain. All hell then breaks loose when several of the rejuvenated dead from *Re-Animator*, including Detective Chapham's wife, fall under the control of Dr. Hill's flying head and attack the lab in an effort to kill West. Detective Chapham, who was killed and reanimated earlier in the film, also joins in the bloody melee. The Bride self-destructs, the lab collapses, and West is borne away by the very half-formed denizens of the dark that he created.

Adaptation

Brian Yuzna, who produced *Re-Animator*, becomes coproducer, director, and co-screenwriter in this sequel. In the opening scenes, he adapts elements of part five of Lovecraft's "Herbert West — Reanimator," in which West and his assistant work as medics in Flanders during World War I. As Lovecraft notes, "West had soon learned that absolute freshness was the prime requisite for useful specimens..." and West makes the point clear in the film that battlefield conditions are most desirable for advancing his experiments in life and death. In both story and film, West injects a dead soldier with the reagent and then has to restrain the living corpse as it remembers and acts out its last moments of battle.

When the scene shifts back to Miskatonic University Medical School, the screenplay largely leaves Lovecraft behind except for two sequences. In the first, a box containing the head of Dr. Hill arrives at West's lab. In the story, the box contains the head of the soldier West decapitated as part of his experiment in Flanders. In both the story and film, chaos breaks loose in the lab, and West is attacked by creatures he constructed of body parts. Lovecraft writes, "West did not resist or utter a sound. Then they all sprang at him and tore him to pieces before my eyes, bearing the fragments away into that subterranean vault of fabulous abomination."

Lovecraft's story, which appeared in the humor magazine *Home Brew*, was meant to satirize the more outlandish horror tales of his time. *Re-Animator* and its sequel could well be viewed as doing the same thing with late twentieth century horror cinema.

Critique

In between the first and last sequences much mayhem and black humor are the rule. For example, one of West's most memorable creations is an eyeball that walks about on fingers. In another scene, the leading lady finds her dog returned to life, only to discover that it extends to her a human arm and hand to shake. There are many dark lines that bring chuckles. For example, West advises Cain, who is chatting up his girlfriend, "Don't let the little head fool the big head, Dan." In another scene, West tickles the foot of a severed leg as the toes twitch in response. The foot kicks West in the face forthwith. Then there is the scene in which Detective Chapham, a walking mess of a corpse with dried blood all over his mouth, enters the house showing his badge for identification and seeks to make an arrest. Finally, we can't forget the scene in which Gloria the Bride disintegrates and West calls to Cain, "Make a note of it Dan. Tissue rejection!" The Bride is actually patterned after Elsa Lanchester in *The Bride of Frankenstein* (1935). Interestingly, the most memorable part of the film for me is when Gloria the Bride cries out in anguish upon being rejected by Cain. Playing completely straight, actress Kathleen Kinmont really makes you feel her pain!

Besides tipping his hat to Lanchester, Yuzna also alludes to George Romero's grim classic, *Night of the Living Dead* (1968). In both *Night* and *Bride of Re-Animator* people find themselves trapped in a room as zombies beat on the door to gain entry. But West faces something worse than Romero's protagonists did. "My God!" West exclaims. "They're using tools!"

As was the case with the original *Re-Animator*, *Bride* relies on the personality and antics of Lovecraft's "cursed, little tow-head fiend, Herbert West," as portrayed by Jeffrey Combs. Abbott and Gale are also quite good in reprising their original roles. Richard Band again affectionately rips off Bernard Hermann's music from *Psycho* and the ubiquitous special effects are appropriately bizarre, over-the-top and sickening. Unfortunately, the screenplay is not as tight as the original.

Brian Yuzna next wanted to direct an adaptation of either Lovecraft's "Shadow over Innsmouth" or "The Thing on the Doorstep" but couldn't get financing. Thus, his next Lovecraft project turned out to be *Necronomicon* (1993).

Rating: 2

The Resurrected (1991)
aka *The Ancestor*, aka *Shatterbrain*

Directed by Dan O'Bannon. Screenplay by Brent V. Friedman, based on *The Case of Charles Dexter Ward* by H.P. Lovecraft. Produced by Mark Borde and Kenneth Raich. Music by Richard Band. Cinematography by Irv Goodnoff. 99 minutes.

Cast: John Terry (John March), Jane Sibbett (Claire Ward), Chris Sarandon (Charles Dexter Ward/Joseph Curwen) Robert Romanus (Lonnie Peck).

Synopsis

Private investigator John March closes the case of Charles Dexter Ward. In flashback we are told why.

Claire Ward hires investigator March to find out what is going on with her husband, Charles Dexter Ward. Charles has purchased a farmhouse near a cemetery. In the adjoining barn, he has set up a laboratory and hired a sinister assistant. Mr. Fenner, a neighbor, complains about strange deliveries made to the lab. The police investigate and find body parts. Vandalism is reported at the cemetery.

It seems that Charles Dexter Ward has become obsessed with the life of his ancestor, Joseph Curwen, an eighteenth century warlock and author of the forbidden tome *To Him Who Shal Come After, How He May Gett Beyonde Time and Ye Spheres*. In the farmhouse, which Curwen once occupied, Ward keeps a portrait of Curwen. The two look remarkably alike.

Fenner is slaughtered and other murders occur. March, his assistant Lonnie Peck, and Claire eventually go into the farmhouse to investigate. Inside, they find an ancient passage leading underground to Curwen's library and to pits where dwell creatures created by Curwen out of "the essential Saltes of humane Dust." It also seems that Ward has summoned forth Curwen himself, and Curwen has taken over Ward's body and identity. Ward is no more. The man believed to be Ward, but who is actually Curwen, is taken away to a mental institution where a demon slaughters him in a padded cell. "The dead take much blood."

And that is why the case of Charles Dexter Ward is closed.

Adaptation

Director Dan O'Bannon (b. 1946) approached Lovecraft's *Case of Charles Dexter Ward* having contributed in various ways to a number of science fiction and horror films. He cowrote John Carpenter's first film, *Dark Star* (1974), wrote *Alien* (1979), cowrote *Dead and Buried* (1981), cowrote Tobey Hooper's *Lifeforce* (1985), wrote and directed *The Return of the Living Dead* (1985), cowrote Toby Hooper's re-make of *Invaders from Mars* (1986), and co-wrote *Total Recall* (1986). At the age of 12, O'Bannon was terrified by Lovecraft's story "The Colour out of Space" and grew up seeing science fiction films such as *The Thing from Another World* (1951) and *Invasion of the Body Snatchers* (1956). O'Bannon considers his first Lovecraft script to be *Alien*, a film that bears a striking resemblance to Jerome Bixby's screenplay for *It! The Terror from Beyond Space* (1958), which in turn bears a striking resemblance to A.E. van Vogt's novel *The Voyage of the Space Beagle*. In an interview with Andrew Migliore and John Strysik, O'Bannon approvingly quotes a Canadian reviewer who wrote, "*Alien* is Lovecraft, but whereas Lovecraft set his stories on earth, *Alien* went to the home planet of the Old Ones."

O'Bannon was considering writing a screenplay based on *The Case of Charles Dexter Ward* when independent producers asked him to direct a screenplay based on the same written by Brent Friedman. In the Migliore and Strysik interview, O'Bannon explained what happened:

> It seemed to me that he [Friedman] didn't make any particular efforts to capture Lovecraft, but simply was putting together a zombish monster movie with teenagers and Lord knows what else. He had some good scenes, but I didn't like the overall shape of it. So I told the producers I would love to direct this film on one condition, we rewrite the script to the plan I have. I put to them what I wanted to do and they all agreed. So under my direction, Brent wrote another draft and we started to film.

O'Bannon's original title for *The Resurrected* was *The Ancestor*. The producers, however, took the film out of O'Bannon's hands, cut scenes, altered sequences, and sent to theaters a retitled version somewhat different from O'Bannon's conception.

What comes to the screen as *The Resurrected* is the most faithful H.P. Lovecraft adaptation yet filmed. Still, there are some key differences. O'Bannon considered Lovecraft's narrator, Dr. Willet, to be one of the most boring characters in fiction and replaced him with private investigator March. In place of the concerned father and mother in Lovecraft's novel, O'Bannon substituted Claire Ward.

In the Migliore and Strysik interview, screenwriter Brent Friedman claims that he wrote his original 1988 screenplay, titled *Shatterbrain* (the Middle English word for "crazy") as "a fairly slavish adaptation of Lovecraft's novelette with Dr. Martin Willet as the main character." His dramatization of Willet's letters provided the screenplay's basic structure. Friedman's original version included deadly doings in the Curwen catacombs, as well as the final confrontation between Willet (later to become Investigator March) and Curwen in the mental institution. Frieman expressed satisfaction with his and O'Bannon's collaboration. He did express regret, however, that they had to cut the concept of Curwen torturing venerable scholars and wizards for their knowledge in the catacombs because the footage proved inferior. Unfortunately, the film is thus missing the explanation of why Curwen had to keep alive his creations, namely that he was still seeking a process that would send them back to ashes.

The theme of Lovecraft's novel is that an ingenious warlock can employ the essential "Saltes" of animals to create living creatures, which require much blood to survive. In the book and film, people and animals disappear near the Curwen-Ward household and are never seen again. In one interesting part of the book, Ezra Ward records in his 1771 diary the abduction of his wife by Curwen. This is shown in the film via flashback. Also in flashback, we see the horror created when some of Curwen's "failures" wash up from the Pawtuxet River. Lovecraft writes that an inhuman creature "half cried out although its condition had greatly departed from that of objects which normally cry out." (When this scene was being filmed in Vancouver, the corpses at one point got away and floated down the river, to be discovered by a couple of very shocked school children playing hooky! When the kids called the cops, the film crew explained the situation, and the kids were duly punished.) As in the book, a complaining neighbor named Fenner and others are killed.

The screenplay places the following eighteenth century–flavored line from the novelette in actor Chris Sarandon's mouth: "I am grown pthisical from this cursed river air," and even borrows lines from Lovecraft's "From Beyond": "I have struck depths your little brain can't picture! I have seen beyond the bounds of infinity and drawn down daemons from the stars.... I have harnessed the shadows that stride from world to world to sow madness and death."

This is not only the most faithful adaptation to date of Lovecraft's *Case of Charles Dexter Ward*, but it also captures much of the novel's theme of necromancy and attendant sense of cosmic horror and nastiness.

Critique

On occasion, a screenplay stays so close to its original source that the film suffers. That is not the case here. The generally faithful screenplay does not slavishly follow the book, which is in many ways unsuitable for cinematic adaptation. Still, one must wonder how improved the film would be had the producers not cut a few original Lovecraft-inspired scenes.

The Resurrected can boast a number of strengths, including Dan O'Bannon's sure direction, cinematographer Irv Goodnoff's eerie use of pale blue tones and dark suggestion, and some terrifying special effects. Acting honors go to Sarandon for his nuanced performance in a dual role and to Robert Romanus as March's likable, efficient assistant.

Of course, this second film version of Lovecraft's novelette invites comparison with the first, Roger Corman's *Haunted Palace* (1963). Briefly, the first version benefits most from the presence of Vincent Price and Lon Chaney, Jr., though Sarandon's Ward/Curwen is slightly superior to that of Price. Ronald Stein's music for *Haunted Palace* is slightly superior to Richard Band's for *The Resurrected*. Special effects for *The Resurrected* dwarf those for *The Haunted Palace*. The supporting cast of *The Haunted Palace* is more memorable that that of *The Resurrected*. All considered, the two films fight to a draw.

Rating: 2½

The Unnamable II: The Statement of Randolph Carter (1992)
Yankee Classic, U.S.A.

Directed by Jean-Paul Ouellette; Produced by Tim Keating; Screenplay by Jean-Paul Ouelette, based on "The Statement of Randolph Carter" by H.P. Lovecraft. 104 minutes.

Cast: Mark Kinsey Stephenson (Randolph Carter), Charles Klausmeyer (Eliot Damon Howard), Maria Ford (Alyda Winthrop), John Rhys-Davies (Professor Warren), Julie Strain (Creature), Peter Breck (Sheriff Hatch), David Warner (Chancellor Thayer).

Synopsis

This film picks up where *The Unnamable* left off. After their encounter with the unknown, Randolph Carter, Howard Damon, and Tanya Heller are escorted to the police station. Along the way, one cop shudders to think, "This might be like that Dunwich thing." At the station, Randolph gives the police his statement and sets off for

Miskatonic University to speak with Professor Warren, the resident expert on the occult. To gain the professor's willingness, Randolph gives the scholar a copy of *The Necronomicon* taken from the Winthrop House. The book is missing important pages.

Professor Warren agrees to help, and the four take flashlights and a wired intercom to Joshua Winthrop's grave. Professor Warren and Randolph descend the steps leading down into the grave and Damon, still recovering from his run-in with Alyda Winthrop, stays above. The three must use the intercom because the earth would block radio transmissions.

Not unexpectedly, Warren and Randolph discover the creature that is Alyda Winthrop, tangled in tree roots as we left her in *The Unnamable*. A quick blood check by Professor Warren reveals that two entities inhabit Alyda's body. The professor proceeds to separate the two entities by administering insulin and sugar cubes. Trailing luminous blue tendrils, the evil entity quickly departs the now lovely, naked body of Alyda Winthrop. Randolph and Howard take Alyda back to their university dorm room where her presence causes a stir among the boys' curious classmates.

Meanwhile, the released demon takes on the form of a creature and goes on a killing spree designed to help it permanently return to the mortal plane. Murdering its way to the dormitory, it hunts for its original host, Alyda. Randolph runs to Miskatonic Library to find the missing pages from *The Necronomicon* in order to combat the she-demon. Unfortunately, when Alyda speaks the ancient language of Cthulhu, he falls into her arms, madly in love. At that moment the she-demon smashes through the window and proceeds to repossess Alyda. In heroic response to the threat, Randolph captures the electrical spirit of the she-demon in a wooden chair. All ends sadly, however, as Alyda, deprived of part of her vital essence, ages rapidly and deteriorates into bone and dust in Randolph's arms.

Adaptation

Very little in this film is adapted from Lovecraft's "The Statement of Randolph Carter." In the story, the narrator, Randolph Carter, makes a statement to the police about the disappearance of his friend Harley Warren. In the film, Carter makes a statement to the police about what happened in the previous film, *The Unnamable*. In the story, Carter holds one end of an intercom as Warren descends to explore a tomb in an ancient, abandoned cemetery. Warren sends up comments such as "God! If you could see what I am seeing!" and "Carter, it's terrible — monstrous — unbelievable!" After a warning from Warren for Carter to "beat it," Warren ceases communication. Alarmed at the developing situation, Carter begins calling, "Warren, are you there?" Then comes a voice that "was deep; hollow; gelatinous; remote; unearthly, inhuman; disembodied." And its shocking message: "YOU FOOL, WARREN IS DEAD!"

In the film, Professor Warren (named after the Lovecraft character) and Randolph Carter descend into the grave connected by intercom with Howard, who remains above. We get nervous communication back and forth as the explorers make their discovery, but, unlike in the story, the two return alive with Alyda in tow. Of course, the film's early reference to Dunwich alludes to other Lovecraft stories such as "The Dunwich Horror." In fact, the creature's rampage as it murders its way back to Alyda in *The Unnamable II* may have been suggested by the monster's murderous trek to Signal Hill in Lovecraft's "Dunwich Horror."

As is the case with most cinematic Lovecraft adaptations, the filmmakers graphically depict what Warren and Carter are seeing in the grave, whereas Lovecraft most effectively leaves whatever dwells below to our imagination.

Critique

This film has its share of liabilities, the most obvious being silliness. For example, when Professor Warren descends into the grave, he happens to take with him a portable microscope which coincidently comes in quite handy. Consider also the idea of separating a demon from a body by injecting insulin and administering sugar cubes! If that isn't enough, the demon's essence is finally trapped in an old wooden chair. This is so unlikely as to seem ridiculous.

Also silly is the decision of the young men to bring Alyda, a beautiful naked woman with long, flowing hair, back to their dorm room. Of course, others are curious. "Oh, my God, that's a naked woman," one exclaims, and another picks up *The Necronomicon* and shouts, "Oh my God, this is quantum physics!"

An additional drawback is the creature itself, which isn't nearly as effective in mannerism this outing as it was when played by another actress in *The Unnamable*. To the film's credit, however, the creature's rampage is fairly rousing. Also to its credit, this sequel avoids the "teenagers being stalked" scenario of its predecessor, which by the time of *The Unnamable* was already hackneyed and predictable. The film has its moments, but not enough to lift this Lovecraft adaptation out of mediocrity.

Rating: 2

Necronomicon (1993)
New Line, U.S.A.

Produced by Samuel Hadida, Taka Ichise, and Brian Yuzna. Music by Daniel Licht and Joseph LoDuca. Edited by Keith Sauter.

"The Drowned": Directed by Christopher Gans. Screenplay by Brent V. Friedman, suggested by "The Rats in the Walls" by H.P. Lovecraft [uncredited]. Cinematography by Russ Brandt.

"The Cold": Directed by Shusuke Kaneko. Screenplay by Kazanore Ito, based on "Cool Air" by H.P. Lovecraft [uncredited].

"Whispers": Directed by Brian Yuzna. Screenplay by Brian Yuzna, based on "The Whisperer in Darkness" by H.P. Lovecraft [uncredited]. 96 minutes.

Cast: (Wraparound) Jeffrey Combs (H. P. Lovecraft), Tony Azito (Librarian).

"The Drowned": Bruce Payne (Edward De La Poer), Richard Lynch (Jethro De La Poer), Denice D. Lewis (Emma De La Poer), Maria Ford (Clara), Peter Jasienski (Jethro's son).

"Cold": David Warner (Dr. Madden), Bess Meyer (Emily Osterman), Millie Perkins (Lena), Dennis Christopher (reporter), Gary Graham (Emily's stepfather).

"Whispers": Signy Coleman (Sarah), Obba Babatunde (Paul), Don Calfa (Mr. Benedict), Judith Drake (Mrs. Benedict).

Synopsis

In the fall of 1932, H.P. Lovecraft visits the library of the Omjahdi monks in order secretly to access a copy of the dreaded *Necronomicon*. The head librarian is suspicious but allows Mr. Lovecraft to examine some innocuous book that the latter has requested as long as he does not venture into other parts of the library. Of course, Lovecraft leaves his assigned space and finds the copy of *The Necronomicon* that he seeks. When Lovecraft removes the book from its cabinet, unknown to him, a portal begins to open. Lovecraft produces a notepad and begins transcribing a story he titles "The Drowned."

In "The Drowned," Edward De La Poer, the last of his line, returns to New England to claim the family estate. Showing him the dilapidated manor is attractive blond Clara, a flirty real estate agent. When Clara departs, Edward examines a letter from his deceased Uncle Jethro, which (in flashback) reveals some disturbing family history. It seems that Jethro, who survived a shipwreck in which his wife and child died, disturbed his friends and neighbors by burning his Bible and denouncing God. Soon after, he was visited by a creature that delivered to him *The Necronomicon*, saying in a sea-drenched tone, "In your time of need, you are not alone."

Jethro opened the book and read, "That which is not dead can eternal lie,/ And with strange aeons even death may die,/ In his lair Cthulhu waits dreaming." Jethro then resurrected the bodies of his dead wife and son by performing a ceremony from *The Necronomicon*. Unfortunately, they proved to be two tentacles of the monstrous Cthulhu, who resided in the depths beneath the estate. Able to take no more, Jethro committed suicide by throwing himself into the sea.

Edward finds *The Necronomicon* and decides to resurrect his own dead wife, and with similar results. What seems to be his returned wife is a shapeshifting tentacle of Cthulhu. Edward takes an axe to the tentacle, which brings Cthulhu crashing up through the floorboards of the mansion, obviously as mad as hell. Thinking fast, Edward brings down a spiked chandelier into the cyclopean creature's eye.

Back in the library, Lovecraft, still oblivious to the opening portal, begins to transcribe a story called "The Cold."

"In the midst of this cruel heat wave, the inhabitants of Boston curse their unbearable lot, while one man alone remains cool, cool but imprisoned by his own desperate devices." A reporter from the *Boston Journal* knocks on an apartment house door and is reluctantly admitted by a young woman. The reporter relates that he is investigating several recent murders with the same modus operandi as murders committed years ago in the apartment house. If the young woman will not talk, the reporter threatens to turn over his theory to the police. Under threat, the young woman identifies herself as Amy Osterman, the daughter of Emily Osterman, who years ago moved to Boston to study flute and escape her stepfather's sexual abuse. Emily rented a room from a woman named Lena and learned that a strange recluse named Dr. Madden lives upstairs. When the stepfather barged in with rape on his mind, Dr. Madden saved Emily by impaling the stepfather's hand with a knife. Dr. Madden, who was attracted to Emily, explained that he was suffering from a rare skin condition that required an "unreasonably cold environment." Indeed, the doctor's room was kept at a very low temperature and Dr. Madden himself was cold to the touch. The doctor actually was preserving his youth by following instructions in *The Necronomicon*. A rather unsavory part of the process, however, was the large amount of spinal fluid that the doctor had to extract from his murder victims.

That night, Emily saw blood dripping from the ceiling and went upstairs to find Dr. Madden and Lena killing a man who appeared to be her stepfather. Emily fainted and woke the next morning to Dr. Madden's explanation that she had been dreaming. Emily figured otherwise, however, when she learned at a diner across the street that her stepfather was found murdered. She confronted Dr. Madden, who become ill and had to be iced down in his bathtub by Emily. The two fell in love and had sex. Later, the jealous Lena threatened to kill either herself or Emily if Emily did not go. Emily left but soon returned when she found herself pregnant. To her horror she interrupted another murder and was shot by Lena. Dr. Madden knocked over some chemicals and started a fire that caused him to gruesomely melt and deteriorate.

The reporter guesses that he is actually speaking to Emily, who has been preserving her own youth with *The Necronomicon*, cold air, and spinal fluid from fresh victims. His knowledge comes too late, however, for Emily has drugged him. Still pregnant with Dr. Madden's baby after all this time, she hopes to someday give birth. Meantime, the baby in her womb has made her like Dr. Madden. As the reporter languishes on the floor, an elderly Lena enters the room with a hypodermic needle. She too wants to see the baby delivered, because it is the offspring of the man she loved.

Back in the library, Lovecraft begins transcribing "Whispers," while the gateway continues to open.

Two cops engage in a high-speed car pursuit of a serial killer known as the Butcher. Amidst the action, female officer Sarah reveals to her partner Paul that she is pregnant with his child. With their attention distracted, their cruiser flips over, and a figure wearing red galoshes drags the badly injured Paul through a broken window.

Sarah sees the galoshes, and, when sufficiently recovered, she follows Paul's trail of blood into an eerie old warehouse. Inside, she encounters the humorous Mr. Benedict, who identifies himself as the owner of the warehouse. He tells Sarah that the Butcher does stay in the building sometimes, but has not been there recently. Going deeper into the building with Mr. Benedict, Sarah encounters blind Mrs. Benedict, who somehow knows that Sarah is pregnant. Mrs. Benedict also owns a copy of *The Necronomicon*, which sits next to her record player. Her hosts tell Sarah that the Butcher is really an alien who has resided on earth since before the days of the dinosaurs.

Mr. Benedict leads Sarah into a tunnel full of Lovecraftian bas-reliefs depicting all sorts of ancient sacrifice and butchery. He then tells Sarah that the Butcher is not an alien, but that he works for aliens, having given up on God and placed his chips on another horse. Then Sarah watches as Mr. Benedict puts on a pair of red galoshes. Just as Sarah realizes that Mr. Benedict is actually the Butcher, Mrs. Benedict torches her and pushes her down a slimy tunnel into a large enclosure full of decaying corpses. Sarah puts out the fire but finds herself in even greater danger. She finds Paul, barely alive, with horrible liquids pouring from his mouth. She is then attacked by bat-like extraterrestrials. Horrors pile upon horrors and Sarah suddenly wakes to find herself in a hospital bed cared for by Mr. and Mrs. Benedict in the form of a doctor and her own mother.

The doctor and Mrs. Benedict tell Sarah she has been unconscious for several days following an accident. Talk turns to the baby Sarah wants to abort, and Sarah's mother informs her that Paul is brain-dead behind a curtain in the room with her. All hell breaks loose as the doctor shows Sarah the grotesque figure of Paul, and her mother reveals visually that she is now carrying Sarah's baby. Sarah is still in the clutches of the Benedicts and is having her marrow sucked by the aliens.

Back in the library, Lovecraft finishes "Whispers." The librarian assaults Lovecraft, planning to feed him to the monster that is approaching from another dimension. Lovecraft unmasks the librarian as an alien and escapes, leaving the latter to be devoured by the monster, which then returns to whence it came. Lovecraft leaves the library by cab. When asked by the cab driver if he found what he was looking for, Lovecraft replies that *it* found *him*!

Adaptation

"The Drowned" is very loosely based on Lovecraft's "Rats in the Walls." In Lovecraft's story, the narrator, a scion of the old English Delapore family, returns from Bolton, Massachusetts, to his English ancestral home at Exham Priory to restore his family estate. He later adopts the original spelling of his family name, De La Poer (with homage to Edgar A. Poe). In the film, Edward, the last descendent of the De La Poer line, returns to New England (not England) to possess and restore his family estate, which is now a rundown hotel. In the film, De La Pore finds the source of the horrors that had afflicted his family under the floorboards of the estate. The horror is the great god Cthulhu itself. The major part of the film, focusing on necromancy and resurrection of the dead, was not of interest to Lovecraft in "The Rats in the Walls."

"The Cold" is an updated yet clearly identifiable adaptation of Lovecraft's "Cool Air." As in most of Lovecraft's work, "Cool Air" has no heroine. The film's Dr. Madden stands in for Lovecraft's Dr. Munoz.

"Whispers" actually borrows as much from "The Rats in the Walls" as it does from "The Whisperer in Darkness." In "Rats in the Walls," the narrator discovers an underground world beneath his house filled with human skeletons and a chronological series of temples arranged for human sacrifice and cannibalism, much as Sarah discovers in truncated form when led by the Benedicts into the depths below the warehouse.

The creatures Sarah encounters in the warehouse grotto are Lovecraft's Mi-Go from "The Whisperer in Darkness." Lovecraft describes them as: "...pinkish things about five feet long; with crustaceous bodies bearing vast pairs of dorsal fins or membranous wings and several sets of articulated limbs, and with a sort of convoluted ellipsoid, covered with multitudes of very short antennae, where a head would ordinarily be." The producers of the film accurately adapt these creature to the screen.

In Lovecraft's story, ancient legends "...unanimously agreed that the creatures were not native to this earth." Also, "there are shocked references to hermits and remote farmers who at some period of life appeared to have undergone a repellent mental change, and who were shunned and whispered about as mortals who had sold themselves to the strange beings. In one of the northeastern counties it seemed to be a fashion about 1800 to accuse eccentrics and unpopular recluses of being allies or representatives of the abhorred things." The film's setting is urban rather than rural, but the Benedicts are such reclusive people who ally themselves with the aliens. As Mr. Benedict tells Sarah when giving his account of the Butcher, "The Butcher is not an alien, but he is working for an alien.... He's bettin' God's a goner, and he's putting all his chips on another horse."

But what are we to make of the film's preoccupation with pregnancy? Human mothers obviously rate pregnancy highly. On the conscious level, women want to bring new life into the world, and on the instinctual level, the preservation of the species is always a natural priority. In the second segment, the screenwriter introduces pregnancy into the adaptation of a story in which pregnancy plays no part, and in the third segment, pregnancy and the threat of abortion is a dominant theme missing from the original story.

In the amateur publication *Nyclatops* (vol. 2, no. 2, 1979), author R. Alain Everts reveals Sonia Lovecraft's own words about her husband's sexuality. According to Everts, Sonia said that Lovecraft knew how to pleasure a woman. Before their marriage, the virginal Lovecraft read up on the subject and was intent on being a good husband in all ways. His Puritanical upbringing and his own mother's insistence on reminding him of his "grotesque" features probably saddled him with a perspective on sex shared by few other men.

The obsession with pregnancy is obviously that of the screenwriter, not of Lovecraft. Still, adapting the theme into an eighties film is understandable since abortion was then and still is a controversial cultural issue.

Critique

The wraparound, of course, is 100 percent wrong in portraying Lovecraft as a believer in the occult. It does, however, provide a fairly coherent and suspenseful introduction to the stories. Special effects are the real star of "The Drowned." The cast and cinematography are competent enough to keep the viewer engaged. The idea of a single human being triumphing over Cthulhu strains credulity while at the same time satisfying human audiences.

The dominant theme of the entire film is very Lovecraftian. The first and third stories allude to Lovecraft's philosophy that human beings are not necessarily the crowns of creation in a disinterested, materialistic universe. The fungi of Yuggoth, malignant by human standards, is simply another life form, from a Lovecraftian perspective.

The third story expertly mixes humor with horror while leaving us with the unmistakable prediction that horror lurks just behind the facade of modern life. The second episode gives us a welcome chance to see Millie Perkins on screen again after a very long layoff. Viewers will remember her in the starring role in *The Diary of Anne Frank* (1959).

Rating: 2½

The Lurking Fear (1994)
Full Moon, U.S.A.

Directed by C. Courtney Joyner. Screenplay by C. Courtney Joyner, based on "The Lurking Fear" by H.P. Lovecraft. Executive producer, Charles Band. Produced by Oana Paunescu and Vlad Paunescu. Music by Jim Manzie. Cinematography by Adolfo Bartoli. 76 minutes.

Cast: Jon Finch (Bennett), Blake Bailey (John Martense), Ashley Laurence (Cathryn Farrell), Jeffrey Combs (Dr. Haggis), Allison Mackie

(Ms. Marlowe), Paul Mantee (Father Poole), Vincent Schiavelli (Knaggs), Joseph Leavengood (Pierce), Michael Todd (creature).

Synopsis

When young, good-looking prison inmate John Martense is paroled, he learns from one of his father's partners, an undertaker named Knaggs, that money left by his deceased gangster father is sewn inside a corpse in the Lefferts Corners Cemetery. Armed with a map, John heads for Lefferts Corners. Soon after, three gangsters, Bennett, Ms. Marlowe, and Pierce, show up at Knaggs' funeral home looking for the map. Under threat, Knaggs decides to cooperate but gets a fatal shot in the gut for his trouble.

At the church and cemetery, a strange plan is unfolding. As night falls and a thunderstorm approaches, alcoholic, chain-smoking Dr. Haggis, Cathryn Farrell, Father Poole, and a pregnant girl prepare to blow up the cemetery in an effort to kill a brood of cannibals living in underground labyrinths. For 20 years these cannibals, the degenerated ancestors of John Martense, have emerged to feed on the flesh of the living during nighttime thunderstorms.

Martense arrives at the cemetery, followed shortly by the gangsters, who gain the upper hand and order Martense to dig up his grandmother's coffin. When the deed is done amidst a pouring rain, the corpse is found to be penniless, at which point a cannibal creature pulls Martense down through a tunnel connected with his grandmother's grave. Martense escapes, but as the evening progresses not everyone is so lucky. Father Poole has his heart ripped out by a cannibal, Pierce is pulled through a window and eaten, and Ms. Marlowe and Bennett are killed when the cemetery explodes, destroying the cannibals.

Adaptation

C. Courtney Joyner's screenplay adapts Lovecraft's theme of an inbred family's degeneration into cannibalism. In Lovecraft's story, however, the cannibals live in secret tunnels under and surrounding the Martense family mansion on Tempest Mountain in the Catskills. In both story and film, the cannibals come out during nighttime thunderstorms to eat their prey. In the story, there are thousands of Martense cannibals, whereas the film reduces the number to six. Finally, the story and screenplay are alike in that both Martense Mansion in the story and the old church in the film are destroyed by explosives.

In Lovecraft's words, when the thunderstorm begins, it calls "the death-daemon out of some fearsome secret place"; this soon happens in the film when long-nailed hands drag Martense down what Lovecraft calls a "burrow of caked loam that stretched and curved." The production crew does a fine job of bringing Lovecraft's descriptions to life.

Lovecraft describes the cannibals as "a loathsome night-spawned flood of organic corruption more devastatingly hideous than the blackest conjuration of mortal madness and morbidity." Later, he gets more specific: "...they were dwarfed deformed hairy devils or apes — monstrous and diabolical caricatures of the monkey tribe. They were so hideously silent; there was hardly a squeal when one of the last stragglers turned with the skill of long practice to make a meal in accustomed fashion on a weaker companion." The film's cannibals are not ape-like. Instead they have thin, stringy white hair and enlarged white eyeballs. In fact, they most resemble the crypt-keeper on television's *Tales from the Crypt.*

Lovecraft's story illustrates his horror of "the other," of foreigners and other races that do not exhibit an understanding or appreciation of the higher culture built by Anglo-Saxon England and America. It is significant that, though generations removed, the cannibals eat their own, the story therefore expressing Lovecraft's fear that foreign cultural and racial elements would infiltrate America in "underground" ways and destroy the host culture.

Of course, Lovecraft's story contains no gangster drama, and no character in the film resembles anyone in the story. This is an inevitable result of having to pad a full length film adapted from a short story. Another difference is that Lovecraft's story has much greater scope than the film. For example, Lovecraft's story describes a whole population of squatters having been wiped out in a single stroke by a thousand or more cannibals. This grand scale could obviously not be replicated on Full Moon's budget.

In an interview with Migliore and Strysik, director and screenwriter C. Courtney Joyner explained that he was asked by producer Charles Band to write a script for one of Full Moon's *Puppet Master* films. Joyner agreed on the condition that he could direct a film in the future. Band said he had a project in mind to do after shooting wrapped on a picture called *Dr. Mordrid*, starring Jeffrey Combs. Joyner ended up directing *Trancers III*, which was a financial success. Band then approached Joyner about directing a sequel, but Joyner said he would prefer to do *The Lurking Fear*, which he knew Full Moon was holding for Stuart Gordon. With a little negotiation, Joyner landed *The Lurking Fear* as his next project.

Joyner was familiar with some of Lovecraft's work based on reading he had done while in high school. He was impressed by the author's "attention to detail and his attempt to describe madness and decay." Joyner realized the difficulty of capturing Lovecraft's mood and essence on film. Many films had failed, and Full Moon had a limited budget.

To cut costs, the film was shot in 28 days in Romania. An old church and its surroundings were already set to be demolished because they had been partially destroyed by the Russians. The assistant director bought the church and the surrounding land, thereby eliminating the need to build artificial sets. Local authorities even allowed them to blow up the buildings at the end of the film. The very important and prominent boarded-up hole in the middle of the church floor was already present when production began. There were some communication problems, however, between the film crew and their Romanian helpers. For example, before doing the scene in which Dr. Haggis drinks sacramental wine, Jeffrey Combs asked the prop man to bring him the bottle of wine. The prop master returned with a corncob.

Joyner complained that he parted company with Full Moon after *The Lurking Fear* because, among other things, the producer allowed someone to edit the film who was already working on two projects. Despite post-production problems, the film turned a profit. This is in no small part attributable to the cast, headed by British leading man Jon Finch (b. 1944) and Lovecraft veteran Jeffrey Combs. Finch was no stranger to horror films, having costarred in Hammer's *The Vampire Lovers* (1970) and *Horror of Frankenstein* (1971), as well as in Roman Polanski's *Macbeth* (1971) and Alfred Hitchcock's *Frenzy* (1972). Joyner had wanted Oliver Reed for the part of Bennett, but Full Moon still owed him money from a previous film. Regardless, Finch fills the bill nicely. (For background on Jeffrey Combs, see the "adaptation" section under *Re-Animator.*)

Critique

The Lurking Fear is a satisfactory product. Lovecraft fans will undoubtedly be put off by liberties taken with the story. Still, the general theme is intact.

Lovecraft aside, the film boasts a very good cast. Jon Finch is particularly impressive as the rough but suave gangster boss, and Jeffrey Combs turns in a performance unlike any of his others in the Lovecraft series. This time he is a frayed, alcoholic medical doctor undoubtedly beaten down by years of tending patients wounded by periodic cannibal attacks. Blake Bailey is adequate as the pretty boy parolee. Vincent Schiavelli, who provides some comic relief, scores as the sleezy undertaker. Paul Mantee, who looks a lot like Tommy Lee Jones, is adequate as the priest, and Allison Mackie does a good job playing a broad in the mode of *Basic Instinct*'s Sharon Stone. Ashley Laurence, who looks a lot like Winona Ryder, is appealing as the tough-as-nails commando babe aiding Dr. Haggis. In fact, one of the film's high points is a climactic martial arts battle between Mackie and Laurence in the cemetery.

Speaking of memorable scenes, the best segment in the film is the pre-credit prologue in which two women and a baby huddle in fear inside their dilapidated house on Christmas Eve. When long-nailed hands reach through a boarded-up vent after the baby, mother goes to the rescue. Unfortunately, though her baby remains safe, the mother is brutally pulled through the bloody vent to her eventual death. In this sequence and in a few others, the cinematographer makes good use of some subjective camera angles from the cannibals' perspective.

In the negative column, the Eastern European setting fails to convey any intended New England atmosphere, and the film would have worked better had it not tried to mix horror and gangster elements. With the possible exception of *Black Friday* (1940), no horror film has mixed those elements successfully. However, *The Lurking Fear* certainly equals or surpasses such attempts as *Creature with the Atom Brain* (1955), *Creature from the Haunted Sea* (1960), and *Beast from Haunted Cave* (1960).

Another problem in the film is that the cannibals aren't presented as an imminent enough threat to build much suspense. Yes, they are around someplace, but they only attack isolated people. To the viewer it seems that if the whole bunch in the church wanted to escape they need only leave. The heroes are staying presumably to make sure that the explosives go off, but it seems they too could have devised a somewhat better plan. Finally, the characters are very sympathetic but uninteresting. Blame the screenplay for this.

Rating: 2

Dagon (2001)
Fantastic Factory, U.S.A.

Directed by Stuart Gordon. Produced by Brian Yuzna and Julio Fernández. Music by Carlos Cases. Cinematography by Carlos Suarez. Screenplay by Dennis Paoli, based on the stories "Dagon" and "The Shadow over Innsmouth" by H.P. Lovecraft. Edited by Jaume Vilalta.

Cast: Ezra Godden (Paul), Francisco Rabal (Ezequiel), Raquel Merono (Bárbara), Macarena Gómez (Uxía), Brendan Price (Howard), Birgit Bofarull (Vicki), Uxía Blanco (Ezequiel's mother), Ferran Lahoz (priest), Joan Minguell (Xavier), José Lifante (desk clerk), Alfredo Villa (Captain Combarro).

Synopsis

Paul, who has recently become a multimillionaire as a result of business dealings, and his wife Bárbara are vacationing on a boat off the coast of Spain with the owners of the boat, Howard and Vicky. Bárbara is disturbed that Paul has trouble leaving business concerns behind as she tries to enjoy the outing. A storm rises and strands the boat on a rock. Vicki's leg is trapped as water rushes in from below. Howard comforts Vicki as Paul and Bárbara embark in a raft for the village on shore.

Arriving on shore, Paul and Bárbara run to a church from which emanates strange singing. The words over the church entrance are "Esoterica Orde de Dagon" (The Esoteric Order of Dagon). Upon their entrance the singing stops and they are greeted by the priest. He takes them to the shore and gets fishermen to take Paul through the storm to the boat. Bárbara is to stay in the village and report the accident to police. The priest, by the way, has webbed fingers.

Bárbara runs to the hotel where she tries unsuccessfully to communicate with the unblinking desk clerk. Presently the priest arrives, and he and the desk clerk abduct Bárbara.

Paul returns to the village after failing to find his friends on the boat. The priest tells Paul that Bárbara has gone for the police and will meet him at the hotel in one hour. Though Paul finds Bárbara's lighter on the hotel desk and is suspicious about her whereabouts, he checks into the hotel anyway. Once in his room, Paul is accosted by the strange denizens of the village, who are part fish and part human. He flees and runs into an old man named Ezequiel, with whom he hides and from whom he demands information. The old man, a drunk, says that he has witnessed the deaths of Vicki and Bárbara. He also pours forth the history of the village to Paul. When he was a child, Ezequiel's father was a fisherman, but business was bad. One Sunday, a sailor barged into the church service and told the congregation that they should stop praying to a god that does not answer their prayers; that he would introduce them to a god that would respond positively. The sailor did just that. The god was Dagon, a deity from the sea; and, as a result of prayer and ritual, the sea plentifully supplied fish and gold. Consequently, the citizens trashed the church, killed the priest, and started using the church for the worship of Dagon. Soon Dagon demanded a sacrifice. The chosen victims were Ezequiel's parents, and the boy was forced to swear allegiance to Dagon forever. Afterward, he became a drunk who the villagers knew no one would believe.

Paul doesn't believe Ezequiel at first, but the old man covers for Paul as he breaks into the house of the only person in the village that owns a car. In the house, Paul finds a young woman, Uxía, in bed. She is the beautiful but fearful apparition he has seen in dreams, a mermaid, a woman from the sea. Paul finds her attractive but feels he cannot give himself to her. He is even more convinced when he pulls back the blankets to reveal octopus legs growing from her torso. Saying that they are destined to be together, Uxía begs Paul to stay, but he rushes out of the house pursued by guards and other fish-like villagers. He takes refuge in a house but is accosted by a fish person. He kills the creature, but much to his disgust, its very human son attacks. It seems that children in the village are born human, but over time they degenerate (or evolve?) into fish beings that can live eternally in the waters beyond the village.

Paul is captured and placed in captivity with Bárbara and Vicki (who are not dead) and Ezequiel. Bárbara, who has apparently mated with Dagon, is carrying his child and wants to die. When they try to escape but are recaptured, Vicki commits suicide. The three survivors are restrained, after which the priest surgically and painfully removes Ezequiel's face, leaving him to die. Bárbara is suspended over a pit and lowered down to be Dagon's mate. Paul escapes, disembowels the priest, and tries to rescue Bárbara from the pit. Unfortunately, Dagon ascends and pulls her into the depths, leaving only her severed arms still hanging from the ropes.

Finally Paul realizes that his and Uxía's mother were the same woman and that their father was Dagon. Paul plunges into the water with Uxía and inhales the water effortlessly. They will live together eternally in the depths of the sea.

Adaptation

Though the credits do not say so, *Dagon* is based primarily on Lovecraft's "Shadow over Innsmouth," which explores the theme of the moral and racial corruption in a human community. The corruption begins in the film, as it does in the story, with a community's loss of faith in Christianity and its replacement with a religion of gods from the deep. Christ certainly has not answered the community's prayers, but they experience immediate reward after converting their Catholic church into a temple for the worship of Dagon and for the practice of human sacrifice.

The narrator in the story stumbles upon Innsmouth under different circumstances than those in the film. In the story, the narrator agrees to take a bus stopping at Innsmouth on the way to Arkham to avoid paying the higher train fare. In the film, Paul, a yuppie multimillionaire, is stranded in a strange village with his girlfriend, Bárbara, after the boat they are on is stranded off the coast of Spain. As usual, a woman, most scarce in Lovecraft's fiction and missing from

"The Shadow over Innsmouth," plays a major supporting role in the film.

In the story, the narrator, a college student, antiquarian, and genealogist, is visiting New England, where his mother was born, and decides to stop for the day in Innsmouth due to curiosity raised by some strange, whispered rumors. As in many Lovecraft stories, curiosity leads the narrator into danger. In the film, Paul simply wants to find his girlfriend and leave as soon as possible. Curiosity sets in only later as an engine of survival. An old, drunken native satisfies the protagonist's curiosity in both story and film. Lovecraft calls him Zadok Allen; the screenwriter calls him Ezequiel, but they are the same memorable person.

The theme of racial degeneration caused by intermarriage probably results in part from Lovecraft's own horror of interracial marriage and his loathing of immigrants (or his love of Western culture). The results of forbidden sex are certainly distasteful, at least from a human standpoint, in both story and film. The transitioning humans sport the "Innsmouth look," bulging fish eyes, receding forehead, and scaly skin. The film's denizen with the slouch hat and trenchcoat is adapted directly from the story, as are other creatures. Paul's beautiful (from the waist up) relative, Uxía, is primarily the creation of the screenwriter, though Lovecraft's narrator does discover that his cousin (by way of Dagon) is an inmate at the Canton mental asylum.

Though Lovecraft felt that he could not write action fiction, the narrator's escape from the Gilman Hotel and his pursuit by the creatures *is* exciting. That excitement and suspense is translated well from story to screen as Paul, with no safe haven, flees the creatures through the village's decaying streets. The ending of both story and film are similar as the protagonist willingly surrenders to the inevitable:

> I shall plan my cousin's escape from the Canton madhouse, and together we shall go to marvel-shadowed Innsmouth. We shall swim out to that brooding reef in the sea and dive down through black abysses to Cyclopean and many-columned Y'hanthlei, and in that lair of the Deep Ones we shall dwell amidst wonder and glory forever.

In the film, of course, Uxía and Paul swim off to eternal bliss, Paul's Bárbara apparently forgotten.

All in all, *Dagon* is a relatively faithful adaptation of "The Shadow over Innsmouth." The settings and time periods are different, and the narrators have different socioeconomic backgrounds and, initially, different motives for their actions. But once the action is centered in the village, the film seriously adapts Lovecraft's basic plot and dominant themes.

Critique

Director Stuart Gordon wanted to film his favorite Lovecraft story, "The Shadow over Innsmouth," after *From Beyond* (1986). He figured he needed about ten million dollars to complete the envisioned project. Horror films were still very popular, partly due to Wes Craven's blockbuster serio-comedy, *Scream* (1996). Gordon found, however, that when he approached studios with his proposal, the human-into-fish scenario elicited more laughs than interest. Gordon got a fairer hearing when he began describing the creatures as "amphibians" rather than fish. Some studios recommended that Gordon make Innsmouth a town of werewolves, but Gordon persevered in holding to Lovecraft.

Gordon's first foray into shooting the film set the action on an island surrounded by a reef off the coast of Massachusetts. At the end, the main character tries to escape by boat but crashes on the reef, after which he is attacked by the underwater creatures. Latex work for the "amphibians," however, proved difficult.

Finally, Gordon temporarily abandoned the project and made *Castle Freak* (1995), a film partially inspired by Lovecraft's "Outsider." Later, Gordon returned to "The Shadow over Innsmouth," shot the film on foreign soil, and released it directly to video. The results are impressive.

The best performance is that of Francisco Rabal, who died shortly after completing the film at the age of 74. Rabal's characterization of a man clinging to sanity in a village where, for mere human beings, very little sanity exists, is both sympathetic and terrifying. In fact, it translates to the screen Lovecraft's fear and loathing of foreign elements growing up around him when he wrote the story. Spanish leading man Rabal, a former electrician, starred in such classic films as Bunuel's *Nazarin* (1959), *Viridiana* (1961), *Belle de Jour* (1961), and

Antonioni's *L'Eclisse* (1962). He also graced Lenzi's graceless horror holocaust, *Incubo sulla Citta Contaminata*, aka *City of the Walking Dead* (1980).

Ezra Godden and Raquel Merono are fine as the young leads, especially Merono, who exudes a definite take-charge sex appeal. Macarena Gómez is impressive as the otherworldly Uxía.

Lovecraft's fish people are skillfully adapted to the screen. Gordon told artist Bernie Wrightson that he wanted both subtle and over-the-top creatures, and Wrightson gave him what he wanted. The artist and monster-maker had previously provided art for Stephen King's *Creepshow* comic book, *The Stand*, *The Cycle of the Werewolf*, and the *TV Guide* cover featuring *The Shining* mini-series.

The underwater photography is good, as is the musical score.

Several scenes in the film are reminiscent of Roger Corman's Lovecraft adaptation *The Haunted Palace* (1963). In Corman's film, Vincent Price and Deborah Paget walk the streets of a village. As they stroll, deformed humans come out into the open and surround them in menacing fashion. Likewise, in Gordon's film, half-human village dwellers lurk in the shadows, arousing fear and suspicion in the protagonists. Corman's finale features a monster rising from a pit to claim its female sacrificial victim. Gordon's film features a similar scene which is more frightening and, as might be expected, technically superior.

Rating: 3

Besides the feature films based on Lovecraft's writings, many amateur filmmakers have tried their hand at adapting Lovecraft's stories. Migliore and Strysik devote 17 pages of their *Lurker in the Lobby* to these efforts. Below is a list of the pieces that they discuss; the interested reader may refer to *Lurker in the Lobby* for further information.

1. *The Whisperer in Darkness* (1975). Super-8MM, 34 minutes. Directed by David C. Smith.
2. *The Haunter of the Dark* (1976). Super-8MM, 14 minutes. Directed by Franklin Hummel.

3. *The Music of Erich Zann* (1980). 16 MM, 17 minutes. Directed by John Strysik.
4. *The Testimony of Randolph Carter* (1988). S-VHS, 30 minutes. Directed by the H.P. Lovecraft Historical Society.
5. *The Outsider* (1993). 16 MM, 8 minutes. Directed by Andrew Hooks.
6. *To Oblivion* (1993). A loose adaptation of Lovecraft's "Ex Oblivione." 16 MM, 12 minutes. Directed by Robert Cappelletto.
7. *The Outsider* (1994). 16 MM, 6 minutes. Directed by Aaron Vanek.
8. *From Beyond* (1997). S-VHS, 10 minutes. Directed by Ken Avenoso and Andrew Migliore.
9. *The Hound* (1997). VHS, 22 minutes. Directed by Anthony Reed.
10. *I Am Providence* (1997). A Lovecraft-oriented documentary of the author's Providence, Rhode Island. Betacam, 28 minutes. Directed by Marcin Gizycki and Agnieszka Taborska.
11. *McLaren* (1997). Inspired by Lovecraft's "Lurking Fear." 16 MM, 8 minutes. Directed by Ted Purvis.
12. *The Case of Howard Phillips Lovecraft* (1998). A "literary and biographic portrait" of Lovecraft. Betacam, 45 minutes. Directed by Pierre Trividic.
13. *From Beyond* (1998). Betacam, 12 minutes. Directed by Magnus Sorell.
14. *The Outsider* (1998). VHS, 6 minutes. Directed by John Allen.
15. *Speaking of the Unspeakable* (1998). A parody of Lovecraft. VHS, 45 minutes. Directed by Jack Reda.
16. *The Unnamable* (1998). Super-8 MM, 22 minutes. Directed by James Fazzaro.
17. *Cool Air* (1999). 16 MM, 44 minutes. Directed by Bryan Moore.
18. *Dagon* (1999). Video, 7 minutes. Directed by Richard Corben.
19. *From Beyond* (1999). DV, 22 minutes. Directed by Bob Fugger.
20. *Return to Innsmouth* (1999). DV, 26 minutes. Directed by Aaron Vanek.
21. *H.P. Lovecraft's Nyarlathotep* (2000). 16 MM, 15 minutes. Directed by Christian Matzke.

Conclusion: The Lovecraftian Cinema

Most of the important horror and science fiction writers were adapted to film as early as their careers allowed. Lovecraft died in 1937, virtually unknown outside of pulp horror fandom. Not until August Derleth founded Arkham House in 1939 and collected Lovecraft's writings did the author gain broader attention. Thereafter, Lovecraft's works became staples in horror anthologies.

The first film adaptations appeared in the 1960s after several popular paperback Lovecraft collections appeared on the market. Even then, the translation of Lovecraft to the screen owed more to Edgar A. Poe and to Hammer Films of England than to anyone else.

Horror cinema changed in 1957 and 1958 with the release of Hammer's *The Curse of Frankenstein* and *Dracula*. The genre was at that time characterized primarily by low budget science fiction films with strong horror elements. Hammer broke the mold by presenting period films shot on relatively low budgets, creating a certain atmosphere and decor that would characterize the "Hammer Universe." The antagonists were often classic horror staples such as Dr. Frankenstein, Dracula, the Phantom of the Opera, and the Mummy, traditional bogeymen in period setting, but presented with a graphic realism missing from their thirties and forties incarnations. Then, in the United States, Alfred Hitchcock's *Psycho* (1960) changed the face of the horror film forever. The monster or the Other was no longer from another country and another time, as was the case in the thirties and forties. Nor as it from outer space. In *Psycho* we met a new monster — and he was us. The monster was the sick human mind in a climate of family breakdown and crumbling traditional values.

Alongside *Psycho*, however, came another new kind of horror film. In 1960, director Roger Corman and American International Pictures launched a series of films loosely based on the writings of Edgar A. Poe. Like Hammer films, these were relatively low budget period pictures that looked opulent to audiences due to great art direction. But they did not feature traditional monsters. The threat in these pictures stemmed from the recesses of a troubled human mind. In that sense they synthesized what was best about Hammer with what was best about *Psycho*. In fact, so different was this sort of picture that some critics have considered the Corman-Poe series to be out of the American mainstream.

Lovecraft entered the horror–science fiction film genre on the coattails of Edgar A. Poe. Corman's *The Haunted Palace* (1963), though based on Lovecraft's "Case of Charles Dexter Ward," was given a Poe title by American International because of the popularity of the ongoing Poe-Corman series. Corman's period pieces had a look and pace that soon became familiar to audiences, as did the repeated starring appearances of Vincent Price. For *The Haunted Palace*, Corman got Vincent Price and Lon Chaney, Jr., and tried to create a Lovecraftian universe as effective as the Poe universe he had created and was developing. AIP changed the name of the film to a Poe title in order to cash in on that series. Poe got the credit, not Lovecraft.

Daniel Haller, Corman's art director, turned director in England to present *Monster of Terror*, aka *Die, Monster, Die* (1965), based on Lovecraft's "Colour Out of Space." Although the film has some eerie Lovecraftian elements and certainly a Lovecraftian plot, Haller places proceedings squarely in a Poesque universe. Haller followed up with *The Dunwich Horror* (1969), probably the most Lovecraftian of all the sixties adaptations. Still, Lovecraft was not an author whose name alone could easily draw audiences to a movie house. That did not occur until Stuart Gordon launched a Lovecraft film series in 1985, beginning with *Re-Animator*, based on Lovecraft's "Herbert West — Reanimator."

Since the sixties, a number of popular paperback Lovecraft collections have competed on the market, the most prominent being that of Ballantine Books, which featured marvelously evocative covers. By the eighties, the world was ready for H.P. Lovecraft. The films of Gordon and his protégés modernized Lovecraft's settings and drenched the stories with buckets of blood and entrails to satisfy a new kind of young filmgoer: the gorehound. As non-Lovecraftian as this may seem, these generally entertaining films helped introduce a new generation of readers to Lovecraft's work.

So what is Lovecraft's film legacy? It may not be very significant, because Lovecraft's more philosophically challenging and chilling viewpoints have rarely been adequately translated to the screen. That, of course, could be said of most horror–science fiction authors. Screenwriters generally are shooting for a mass audience; therefore, their work cannot be very cerebral. Demographics suggest that the vast audience for horror–science fiction films are adolescents; requiring that screenplays advance the action and keep the jaded moviegoer entertained as he nuzzles with his girl and eats popcorn. This was not true in the twenties, thirties, or forties, but it became a fact beginning in the late fifties and has remained so ever since with only a few notable exceptions.

For example, no Lovecraft film to date has adequately captured the author's materialistic sense of the universe and his view of humanity's smallness and insignificance in the face of a vast, indifferent universe. A few have tried, but they only suggest. Only a few films inspired by Lovecraft, but not based directly on his writings, have done so (e.g., *The Thing* [1982]).

Another underlying Lovecraft theme is unmarketable and politically incorrect today, though voices are rising in its support. That is Lovecraft's view that a once great culture was deteriorating due to an influx of outsiders. Polls show today that a significant majority of Americans fear the increase in legal and illegal aliens. In addition, most Americans are frightened by terrorism, which is insidious. It is not the same kind of enemy as an identifiable country. In the current atmosphere, Lovecraft's parable, "The Shadow over Innsmouth," should translate well onto film, as indeed did Stuart Gordon's *Dagon*. While presenting Lovecraft's ideas on mass market theater screens would conceivably draw large audiences whose fears would be addressed by those themes, it is unlikely that major production companies will take the risk of being labeled racist and xenophobic.

PART FOUR

Films Suggested
or Influenced by
Lovecraft's Works

The following is a filmography of motion pictures noticeably influenced by Lovecraft but not credited to him.

The Thing from Another World (1951)
Winchester Pictures, U.S.A.

Directed by Christian Nyby. Produced by Howard Hawks. Screenplay by Charles Lederer, based on "Who Goes There?" by John W. Campbell, Jr. Cinematography by Russell Harlan. Music by Dimitri Tiomkin. 86 minutes.

Cast: Kenneth Tobey (Captain Patrick Hendry), Margaret Sheridan (Nikki Nicholson), Robert Cornthwaite (Dr. Arthur Carrington), James Arness (The Thing), George Fenneman (Dr. Redding), Dewey Martin (crew chief), and Douglas Spencer (Scotty).

John W. Campbell, editor of *Astounding Stories*, which first published Lovecraft's "At the Mountains of Madness" in 1935, was almost certainly influenced by the latter when he wrote "Who Goes There?,"

121

the direct inspiration for *The Thing from Another World*. In both stories, an Antarctic expedition discovers life from another planet in the frozen north. In both stories, the discovered life form is unconcerned with existence from a human perspective. An examination of the two stories reveals stylistic parallels as well; Campbell is clearly under Lovecraft's spell.

In the film, Captain Hendry leads an expedition to the Antarctic to investigate a reported UFO crash (or landing). Upon arriving, the expedition discovers a saucer buried in the ice and removes the vehicle's only occupant in a chunk of ice. Later, when the chunk of ice is mistakenly melted, the thing inside emerges and goes looking for food, which in this case is human blood. Howard Hawks, who actually directed the film but gave the credit to his editor, creates a claustrophobic, forbidding atmosphere, raises questions of humanity's place in the universe, and in the process creates one of the greatest horror–science fiction films of all time.

Rating: 4

Night Tide (1963)
AIP, U.S.A.

Directed by Curtis Harrington. Produced by Aram Katarian. Original story and screenplay by Curtis Harrington. Music by David Raksin. Cinematography by Vilis Lapenieks. Edited by Jodie Copelan. 84 minutes.

Cast: Dennis Hopper (Johnny Drake), Linda Lawson (Mora), Luana Anders (Ellen Sands), Gavin Muir (Captain Samuel Murdock).

Johnny Drake is a lonely young sailor who meets Mora, a mysterious, attractive girl, on an amusement pier. Johnny learns that Mora works as "The Girl in a Fish Bowl" at a boardwalk concession on the pier. Her boss, Captain Murdock, warns Johnny that Mora is dangerous. Johnny investigates and learns the story that Captain Murdock reared Mora from childhood and that she is a descendant of a mysterious race of sea people who under the spell of the full moon desire to kill.

This plot could easily have been influenced by Lovecraft's "Shadow over Innsmouth" and other such tales. It also seems to borrow a bit from producer Val Lewton's *The Cat People* (1942), in which a man is torn between two women, one with dangerous propensities.

Dark Intruder (1965)
Universal, U.S.A.

Directed by Harvey Hart. Produced by Jack Laird. Screenplay by Barré Lyndon. Music by Lalo Schifrin. Cinematography by John F. Warren. 59 minutes.

Cast: Leslie Nielsen (Brett Kingsford), Mark Richman (Robert Vandenburg), Judi Meredith (Evelyn Lang), Gilbert Green (Harvey Misbach), Charles Bolender (Nikola), and Werner Klemperer (Professor Malaki).

Dark Intruder was originally filmed as a pilot for a television series that never materialized. The film was subsequently released to theaters. The plot concerns Brett Kingsford, an expert in the occult, who quietly offers his help to the police in solving a series of murders. It seems that mummified flesh-and-bone figurines are being discovered near the bodies of victims apparently torn apart by some wild animal. Kingsford opines that "gods older than the human race ... deities like Dagon and Azathoth" still have worshippers. This is the primary and maybe the only link between Lovecraft and the film.

It turns out that all of the victims were members of an archeological expedition to the Middle East and that Kingsford's best friend, Robert, goes into a trance before each murder. Further investigation proves that a member of the expedition delivered twins. One was terribly deformed and left to die. Someone showed pity, however, and saved the child's life. Now, the living twin seeks revenge on all those in the expedition and plans to take over the body of his twin, Robert, by occult means. The evil twin actually succeeds in carrying out his plan, but Kingsford understands that his friend Robert is now the evil twin and kills him.

Although its links with Lovecraft are minimal, the film is quite entertaining and is above average for intended television fare.

Rating: 3

Alien (1979)
20th Century Fox, U.S.A.

Directed by Ridley Scott. Produced by Ronald Shusett. Screenplay by Dan O'Bannon and Ronald Shusett. Music by Jerry Goldsmith. Cinematography by Derek Vanlint. Alien design by H.R. Giger. 116 minutes.

Cast: Sigourney Weaver (Ripley), Tom Skerritt (Dallas), Veronica Cartwright (Lambert), Harry Dean Stanton (Brett), John Hurt (Kane), Ian Holm (Ash), and Yaphet Kotto (Parker).

What were the influences for *Alien*, a film in which a vicious alien life form invades a manned spacecraft in deep space? Many claim that the chief influence is *The Voyage of the Space Beagle* by A.E. van Vogt. Others point to Jerome Bixby's screenplay for *It! The Terror from Beyond Space* (1958). Now, some point to H.P. Lovecraft as a source. It seems clear that Lovecraft is a source, though he may have been filtered through van Vogt and Bixby in the process. Certainly the film depicts a life form (a monster from our perspective) that doesn't give a rip about humanity. It wants to survive as any of us would want to survive in a hostile environment. We can only imagine spiders in their webs discussing how to avoid the onslaughts of humans who for one reason or another hate their very existence. Other life forms look different, act differently, and have their own agendas. *Alien* captures that theme about as well as any film to date, with the possible exception of *The Thing* (1982). Someday, perhaps, we will see the ugly alien win. That would be a shock to cinema audiences indeed, and one that they well should suffer.

Rating: 3

The Fog (1980)
Avco Embassy Pictures, U.S.A.

Directed by John Carpenter. Produced by Debra Hill. Screenplay by John Carpenter and Debra Hill. Music by John Carpenter. Cinematography by Dean Cundey. 89 minutes.

Cast: Adrienne Barbeau (Stevie Wayne), Jamie Lee Curtis (Elizabeth Solley), Janet Leigh (Kathy Williams), John Houseman (Mr. Machen), Tom Atkins (Nick Castle), James Canning (Dick Baxter), and Charles Cyphers (Dan O'Bannon).

Director and screenwriter John Carpenter has expressed in interviews Lovecraft's influence on his career. Carpenter read his first two Lovecraft stories in a Modern Library Giant titled *Great Tales of Terror and the Supernatural.* The two stories were "The Dunwich Horror" and "The Rats in the Walls."

The Fog tells the story of a centennial celebration memorializing a fogbound shipwreck against Arkham Reef. The crew drowned, but legend has it that when the fog returns to Antonio Bay, the dead will rise up and search for the light that led them to their doom. As we learn later in the film, the ship was manned by a group of lepers hoping to set up a colony on the land that became Antonio Bay. The ship also carried a fortune in gold. A group of conspirators, headed by a Father Malone, lured the ship onto the reef with a false light, watched the crew die, stole the gold, and established the community of Antonio Bay.

The fog rolls in on the day of the celebration, and all hell breaks loose, including ghostly figures stepping out of the luminous fog to kill residents of the town. An old diary discloses that the ghosts will return to the sea upon retrieving their gold. This they finally accomplish, after which they kill a priest, the living relative of the man who organized the crime 100 years ago. Then the fog and its ghostly denizens roll back to sea.

The film's merits include a stellar cast, foreboding music by Carpenter, eerie, evocative cinematography by Cundey, and a truly Lovecraftian atmosphere. The past cannot be escaped as an ancient book reveals crimes that must be avenged. Christianity is powerless as the curse unfolds. Indeed, the lead conspirator was a priest, as is his grandson, who pays with his life to balance the scales.

Rating: 3

Paura nella città dei morti viventi (1980) aka *The Gates of Hell*

Dania Film/Medusa International Cinematografica, Italy

Directed by Lucio Fulci. Produced by Robert E. Warner. Screenplay by Lucio Fulci and Dardano Sacchetti. Music by Fabio Frizzi. Special effects by Gino de Rossi. 92 minutes.

Cast: Christopher George, Catriona MacColl, Carlo de Mejo, Janet Agren, and Antonella Interlenghi.

A priest's suicide manages to open the gates of hell on All Saint's Day. On a cemetery stone are the following words:

THE SOUL THAT
PINES FOR ETERNITY
SHALL OUTSPAN
DEATH. YOU
DWELLER OF THE
TWILIGHT VOID COME
DUNWICH

It seems that the village of Dunwich was built over the ruins of Salem, where the infamous witch trials took place. Except for the Lovecraftian gravestone inscription and the town's being named Dunwich, little else Lovecraftian is apparent.

On All Saint's Day, those who are trying to prevent the dead from walking on Earth are frustrated. This is a very gruesome film that turns the stomach. It is also reasonably effective. Fulci creates suspense in the film's first half, and delivers the goods by way of people's skulls being crushed from behind, twisting out hair, skull, and brains. In one of the film's most repulsive scenes, rats congregate to eat the brain from a newly opened skull.

In another memorable scene, an outraged father forces his son to experience a powered drill entering one side of his head and emerging through the other.

In yet another memorable moment, the people in a house are covered with maggots that fly in through the window and cover the room. Interestingly, the people do not turn away in defense but allow the cameramen to feast on their completely exposed, maggot-infested faces.

This is Fulci at his stomach-turning best, but it isn't Lovecraft.
Rating: 2

E tu vivrai nel terrore!— *L'aldilà* (1981) aka *L'aldilà*, aka *You'll Live in Terror*, aka *The Beyond*
Fulvia Film, Italy

Directed by Lucio Fulci. Produced by Fabrizio de Angelis. Screenplay by Giorgio Mariuzzo, Dardano Sacchetti, and Lucio Fulci. Cinematography by Sergio Salvati. Special effects by Germano Natali and Gianetto de Rossi. 90 (86) minutes.

Cast: Katherine MacColl, David Warbeck, Sarah Keller, Antoine Saint-John, Veronica Lazar, Anthony Flees, Giovanni de Nava, and Michele Mirabella.

For some reason, goremeister Lucio Fulci liked to adapt a few Lovecraftian references into his screenplays and then make a completely un-Lovecraftian movie. This he did with *Paura nella città dei morti viventi* (1980) and here he does it again. This time, Fulci includes in his plot *The Book of Eibon*, which was actually the brainchild of author Clark Ashton Smith as part of the Cthulhu Mythos. In the film, the book contains the secret of the seven doors to hell. In 1981 a woman inherits a Louisiana hotel where, in 1927, an artist was crucified after entering hell and painting its landscapes and denizens. This, of course, may have been suggested by Lovecraft's "Pickman's Model." Zombies soon emerge from hell, and Fulci is off and running with another gore fest.

If we leave Lovecraft and Smith aside, the real influences for this film are *The Sentinel* (1976) and *Dawn of the Dead* (1979).

Creepshow, segment "Weeds" (1982)
aka "The Lonesome Death of Jordy Verrill"
Warner Brothers, U.S.A.

Directed by George A. Romero. Produced by Salah M. Hassanein and Richard P. Rubinstein. Segment screenplay by Stephen King. Cinematography by Michael Gornick; Music by John Harrison. 120 minutes.

In his critique of the modern horror tale, *Danse Macabre*, bestselling author Stephen King admitted to admiring H.P. Lovecraft, especially the classic tale "The Colour Out of Space." In 1982, director George A. Romero (*Night of the Living Dead*, 1968) gave King the chance to offer homage to Lovecraft.

In King's screenplay, Jordy Verrill, played by King himself, is a slow-witted country bumpkin amazed by the landing of a meteorite on his farmland. Verrill first considers the financial possibilities the event promises, but soon becomes afraid when an otherworldly growth from the meteorite begins to envelop the farm, and eventually Jordy. The bumpkin rushes about in a state of confusion before finally deciding on the only way out — suicide.

King's slapstick performance, including outlandish overacting, relieves the segment of any horror suggested by Lovecraft.

Rating: Film 2, segment 2

The Evil Dead (1981)
aka *Book of the Dead*
Renaissance Pictures, U.S.A.

Directed by Sam Raimi. Produced by Bruce Campbell, Sam Raimi, and Robert Tapert. Music by Joseph LoDuca. Cinematography by Tim Philo. 85 minutes.

This successful horror film was shot on a shoestring budget over three or four years by fledgling filmmaker Sam Raimi. It proved to be a great success. This being said, the Lovecraft element is slight. Five students retreat to a secluded mountain cabin where they discover the dreaded *Necronomicon* and a tape recording warning any listener not to mess with the book. A foolish attempt to perform an incantation unleashes unearthly forces. Soon the students are turning one by one into zombies. In this case, a borrowing from Lovecraft leads to a wild, effective horror film. This film spawned two sequels: *The Evil Dead II* (1987) and *Army of Darkness* (1993), neither of which capture the quality of the first.

Rating: 3

PART FIVE

Lovecraft on Television

Lovecraft is more adaptable to television than to any other visual medium. Feature films try to bloat his works and often completely misrepresent them. Television's 30-minute time slots offer a great medium for Lovecraft's short stories. Unfortunately, there have been only two straight Lovecraft adaptations.

LOVECRAFT ADAPTATIONS

1. *Night Gallery* (December 1, 1971)

"Pickman's Model." Directed and produced by Jack Laird. Screenplay by Alvin Sapinsley. Makeup by John Chambers. **Cast:** Bradford Dillman (Richard Pickman), Louise Sorel (Mavis Goldsmith), Donald Moffat (Uncle George).

The adaptation sets Lovecraft's 1926 story in 1896. (Backdating Lovecraft is much more successful than updating him, to which much of this book will attest.) In the television tale, Richard Pickman disappears after painting some gruesome pictures, including *Ghoul Preparing to Dine*. Two men, Eliot and Larry, are trying to discover what happened to Pickman and, if possible, find some of his lost pictures. A flashback shows us that the debonair Pickman was dismissed from a position as an art teacher at an art school for rich Boston debutantes. Although Pickman's work fascinates young Mavis Goldsmith, the appalled head of the school discontinues the painter's services. Miss Goldsmith follows Pickman to a tavern after his final class and tries to question him further. Pickman tries to discourage her by stating flatly that he has no use for "human company." When she persists, Pickman reluctantly tells her he is presently working on a series of paintings depicting "a legend which tells of an eldritch race more foul and loathsome than the putrid slime that clings to the walls of hell ... who live deep beneath the earth in dark tunnels, surfacing in the dead of night to practice their unspeakable acts and breed their filthy spawn until the day arrives when their swollen numbers will finally arise and ravish the earth like a noxious plague."

In his haste to escape, Pickman leaves one of his paintings, *Ghoul Preparing to Dine*, in the tavern. Miss Goldsmith takes the painting and discusses it with her uncle George. He explains that legends do exist of a horrible race of ghouls that live underground and surface occasionally to abduct women for purposes of procreation.

From a painting, Miss Goldsmith learns the location of Pickman's secret studio and goes there to return his painting. Upon arriving, she finds no one home. Forcing her way in, she enters Pickman's garret and finds a series of terrifying paintings. Suddenly the gaslight fades, strange noises are heard in the darkness, and red eyes follow her about.

In the nick of time, Pickman returns and orders Miss Goldsmith out for her own good. In exasperation, she finally confesses that she is in love with him. Preoccupied and apparently unmoved by her words, Pickman excitedly orders her out. Then, without explanation, he grasps a club and leaves her alone in the garret. While there, she examines two paintings, one of a hideous creature carrying off a woman and the other of the woman standing beside an ominous child who resembles Pickman. Meanwhile, she can hear the painter's voice ordering something back down into the cellar.

A major struggle ensues, followed by the appearance of one of the monsters from Pickman's paintings. When it tries to carry off the terrified Miss Goldsmith, Pickman tries to rescue her. To her horror, however, Pickman's glove comes off, revealing a claw. All three tumble from a balcony, allowing Miss Goldsmith to escape screaming into the street. The ghoul, deprived of Miss Goldsmith, carries off Pickman instead. Later, when Uncle George opines that Pickman must have been insane, Miss Goldsmith corrects him, saying, "No! He painted what he saw."

The story returns to the present (1896) and the two men decide to open a bricked aperture in the cellar. Below them, the ghoul waits in expectation of being loosed once again.

Lovecraft describes the creatures as "dog-like things," and suggests that their origin might be associated with ancient Salem. The painting, entitled *Ghoul Feeding* in the original story, depicts "a colossal and nameless blasphemy with glaring red eyes, [that] held in bony claws a thing that had been a man, gnawing at the head as a child nibbles at a stick of candy. Its position was a kind of crouch, and as one looked one felt that any moment it might drop its present prey and seek a juicier morsel." Although short and stocky rather than colossal, the television creature is quite in line with Lovecraft's description. Lovecraft suggests that the creatures may have originated in ancient Salem, but the television adaptation suggests origins more akin to the Cthulhu Mythos. Although the adaptation is quite Lovecraftian, there is no Miss Goldsmith or Uncle George in the original story. The most Lovecraftian scene in the adaptation is the one in which Miss Goldsmith is surrounded in the dark by Lovecraft's "mole-like scrambling" and red eyes.

Makeup man John Chambers earned an Emmy nomination for Outstanding Achievement in Make-Up for his rendition of the monster. On the whole, this is the best thing associated with Lovecraft ever produced for television.

2. *Night Gallery* (December 8, 1971)

"Cool Air." Directed by Jeannot Szwarc; Teleplay by Rod Serling, based on "Cool Air" by H.P. Lovecraft. Cinematography by Leonard J. Louth. Art direction by Joseph Alves, Jr. **Cast:** Barbara Rush (Agatha Howard), Henry Darrow (Dr. Juan Munoz), Beatrice Kay (Mrs. Gibbon), Larry Blake (Mr. Crowley), and Karl Lukas (iceman).

Agatha Howard arrives at Mrs. Gibbon's boarding house in search of Dr. Juan Munoz. Agatha's father has died and she wants to notify Dr. Munoz, who worked with her father years ago at MIT. Agatha finds Dr. Munoz a very charming, middle-aged man. His work concerns preserving life after death by virtue of the human will. Dr. Munoz explains that he has an illness that requires he keep his rooms below 55 degrees at all times. As a result, he never ventures out of those rooms. Moved by Dr. Munoz's loneliness and isolation, Agatha begins visiting him regularly and greatly enjoys his company.

During a summer heat wave, Agatha gets a late-night phone call at her hotel. It is Dr. Munoz. The machine that keeps his rooms cool has broken down, and he is desperate for help. A repairman is unable to help, so Agatha has ice delivered to the rooms. All the while, Dr. Munoz is covered from head to foot with a white robe, only his right eye visible. Finally, when all has failed, Dr. Munoz tells Agatha that his wife committed suicide years ago because she could not stand living with a corpse. Dr. Munoz himself died ten years ago and has been preserving his existence with his will and with cool air. He collapses to the floor dead, revealing to Agatha his putrid corpse.

Agatha, who had fallen in love with Dr. Munoz, now visits his grave once every year. His tombstone reads:

Juan Munoz
Born 1877
Died 1913
and 1923

In Lovecraft's story, the male narrator meets Dr. Munoz after suffering a serious heart attack. Serling makes the narrator a woman and turns out a touching love story tinged with horror.

TELEVISION EPISODES WITH LOVECRAFTIAN REFERENCES

1. *Star Trek* (November 20, 1966)

"What Are Little Girls Made Of? Directed by James Goldstone. Screenplay by Robert Bloch. Music by Alexander Courage and Gerald Fried. **Cast:** William Shatner (Captain James Kirk), Leonard Nimoy (Dr. Spock), DeForest Kelley (Dr. Leonard "Bones" McCoy), George Takei (Lt. Sulu), Jimmy Doohan (Scotty), Majel Barrett (Nurse Christine Chapel), Michael Strong (Dr. Corby), Ted Cassidy (android), Sherry Jackson, and Harry Basch.

This episode owes nothing to Lovecraft by way of story. Dr. Corby, the fiancé of Nurse Chapel, is producing a race of androids with which to conquer the universe. Corby hopes to replace Captain Kirk with a mechanical double. Screenwriter and Lovecraft correspondent Robert Bloch sneaks in a mention of "The Old Ones," an obvious reference to Lovecraft. But that is as far as it goes.

2. *Night Gallery* (September 15, 1971)

"Miss Lovecraft Sent Me." Directed by Gene Kearney. Screenplay by Jack Laird. **Cast:** Sue Lyon (Betsy) and Joseph Campanella (vampire).

In this three-and-a-half minute tale, babysitter Betsy, a typical gum-chewing teenager, shows up unawares at the home of a vampire to look after his offspring. She has been sent to the house by a babysitting agency run by a Miss Lovecraft. The vampire goes upstairs to get his child ready, not for bed, but to feed. Betsy, however, sees a series of books titled *Vampyricon, Satan's Invisible World Discovered, The Book of the Dead, Men to Wolf,* and *The Necronomicon.* Betsy has seen enough, and, exercising grand judgment for a gum-chewing teenager, runs from the house. Except for the name of the babysitting agency, the only reference to Lovecraft is *The Necronomicon.* The episode is mildly humorous, so who is to complain?

3. *Night Gallery* (November 10, 1971)

"Professor Peabody's Last Lecture." Directed by Jerrold Freedman. **Cast:** Carl Reiner (Professor Peabody).

Professor Peabody gives a lecture about the Elder Gods, making fun of them at every turn. In the lecture hall, however, are students Robert Bloch and August Derleth, who pose questions as to the possible reality of the gods that Peabody mocks. Those gods are (on the blackboard) Nyarlathotep, Umrat-tawil, Great Hastur, Cthulhu, Rlyteh Cthulhu, Azathoth, Shub-Niggurath, and Yog-Sothoth.

As Peabody continues his "humorous" lecture, the skies darken and the heavens quake. Suddenly Peabody is struck dead by powers from beyond, turning him into something possibly recognizable by readers of Lovecraft's "Colour out of Space."

This is a quite humorous tale that does justice to Lovecraft and introduces viewers to part of the Lovecraft pantheon of gods. It is doubtful, however, that many viewers in 1971 got the joke, since the Lovecraft paperbacks were just beginning to appear. Regardless, this is a good show indeed.

4. *Real Ghostbusters* (1988)

"The Collect Call of Cathulhu *[sic]*. Written by Michael Reaves.

This campy cartoon begins with tentacles stealing *The Necronomicon* from the New York Public Library. When such things happen, "who you gonna' call?" The answer, of course: Ghostbusters. According to the ghostbusters, Lovecraft penned a "whole series of horror stories" involving *The Necronomicon*. At the library, the investigators encounter Professor Ted Klein (a play upon horror author T.E.D. Klein) and Clark Ashton (a play upon Clark Ashton Smith). The ghostbusters finally meet the spawn of "Cathulhu" in the New York sewers. Realizing they need more knowledge than they have, the ghostbusters interview a Miskatonic University occult scientist named Alice Derleth (a play on August Derleth). The whole affair finally comes to an end (none too soon) when the ghostbusters destroy the risen "Cathulhu" with electricity and uncover Clark Ashton as the villain behind the scenes.

5. *Witch Hunt* (1994), HBO Made-for-Television Film

Directed by Paul Schrader. Produced by Gale Anne Hurd and Michael R. Joyce. Coproduced by Betsy Beers. Music by Angelo Badalamenti. Cinematography by Jean-Yves Escoffier. Screenplay by Joseph Dougherty. **Cast:** Dennis Hopper (Detective Harry Phillip Lovecraft), Ann Miller (Kim Hudson), Eric Bogosian (Larsen Crockett), Sheryl Lee Ralph (Hypolita Kroptkin), Alan Rosenberg (Gottlieb), and Julian Sands (Finn Macha).

This sequel to HBO's *Cast a Deadly Spell* owes very little to H.P. Lovecraft except for the name of the main character, played by Dennis Hopper. Detective Lovecraft is hired by actress Kim Hudson to trail her philandering studio husband, Gottlieb, who soon dies a strange death. Interestingly, witchcraft is openly acknowledged and practiced at this time; for instance, the studio is hiring occult practitioners to cast spells. In this strange milieu, a crusading senator, in the mold of Hollywood's conception of Senator Joseph McCarthy, is trying to outlaw magic. We can only assume he is succeeding, since there is little magic in this made-for-television oddity except for some engrossing special effects. Oh, yes. Detective Lovecraft does utter one very memorable line: "If God doesn't destroy Hollywood, He owes Sodom and Gomorrah an apology."

6. *Superman* (October 6, 1997)

"The Hand of Fate."

Dr. Fate, a golden-age pulp hero, aids Superman in combating Karkall, a demon that has opened a gate to beyond through which other Cthulhu-like demons invade the earth. Dr. Fate comes to the rescue when the invaders possess Lois Lane and Jimmy Olson.

PART SIX

Lovecraft in Comic Books

A black and white comic book, when compared to a color comic book deserves the same consideration as a black and white film deserves when compared to a color film. Early films were made in black and white because there was no alternative. Later, some directors chose to shoot in black and white even though color was available. Usually, the decision was based on finances. The same can be said of comic books. To keep prices down and sales up, some comic books have chosen to offer black and white stories behind color covers. A good film is a good film, and a good comic is a good comic, regardless of color or the lack of. Comic book artists are to their product as cinematographers are to theirs. They decide what the viewer will see as the story unfolds.

Whether a comic is in color or in black and white will not play a great roll in whether one enjoys the comic or not. All the following comic books are in full color unless otherwise stated. All the books have color covers.

Lovecraft's greatest horrors (or monsters) do not adapt well to visual depictions, as most Lovecraft film adaptations prove. The payoffs, so to speak, are always disappointing compared to what the reader might imagine based on Lovecraft's prose. The same applies to comic books to even a greater extent than to films.

Still, the comic book adaptations are purer adaptations than we often get on film or on television. The writers are much more interested

137

in faithfully conveying Lovecraft to the reader than film and television producers are. Most of the comic books listed offer straight adaptations, and to repeat the plots would simply be to repeat the story plots, already briefly done in an earlier chapter. Readers of Lovecraft will be happy to know that most adaptations include direct quotations from Lovecraft's writings.

1. *Vault of Horror* No. 16 (December 1950–January 1951). EC.

"Fitting Punishment." Adapted by Ingels and Al Feldstein, from "In the Vault" by H.P. Lovecraft.

2. *Vault of Horror* No. 17 (February–March 1951). EC.

"Baby, It's Cold Outside." Adapted by Ingels and Al Feldstein, from "Cool Air" by H.P. Lovecraft.

3. *Creepy* No. 21 (July 1968). Marvel. Black and white.

"The Rats in the Walls." Adapted by Bob Jenney, from the story by H.P. Lovecraft.

4. *Chamber of Darkness* No. 5 (June 1970). Marvel.

"The Music from Beyond." Adapted by Roy Thomas and Johnny Craig, from "The Music of Erich Zann" by H.P. Lovecraft.

5. *Tower of Shadows* No. 3 (January 1970). Marvel.

"The Terrible Old Man." Adapted by Roy Thomas, Barry Smith, Dan Adkins, and John Verpoorten, from the story by H.P. Lovecraft.

6. *Tower of Shadows* No. 9 (January 1971). Marvel.

"Pickman's Model." Adapted by Roy Thomas and Tom Palmer, from the story by H.P. Lovecraft.

7. *Skull Comics* No. 4 (1972).

"Cool Air." Adapted by M.C.S., from the story by H.P. Lovecraft.

"The Hound." Adapted by Jaxon, from the story by H.P. Lovecraft.

"Pickman's Model." Adapted by Herb Arnold, from the story by H.P. Lovecraft.

8. *Skull Comics* No. 5 (1972).

"The Rats in the Walls." Adapted by Richard Corben, from the story by H.P. Lovecraft.

"The Shadow from the Abyss." Adapted by Todd, from "The Shadow out of Time" by H.P. Lovecraft.

"To a Dreamer." Adapted by C. Dallas.

9. *Journey into Mystery* No. 4 (April 1973). Marvel.

"The Haunter of the Dark." Written by Ron Goulart, based on a story by H.P. Lovecraft. Artwork by Gene Colan. Inks by Dan Adkins.

10. *Masters of Terror* Vol. 1, No. 2 (September 1975). Marvel.

"The Music from Beyond." First appeared in *Chamber of Darkness* No. 5 (June 1970).

"The Terrible Old Man." First appeared in *Tower of Shadows* No. 3 (January 1970).

"Pickman's Model." First appeared in *Tower of Shadows* No. 9 (January 1971).

11. *Heavy Metal* Vol. 3, No. 6 (October 1979). Black and white.

"The Dunwich Horror." Adapted by Breccia, from the story by H.P. Lovecraft.

"The Thing." Adapted by Voss, from "The Statement of Randolph Carter" by H.P. Lovecraft.

12. *Creepy* No. 113 (November 1979). Black and white.

"Cool Air." Adapted by Bernie Wrightson.

13. *Fantasy Empire Presents H.P. Lovecraft* (1984). Black and white.

"The Festival." Adapted by Bruce McCorkindale, from the story by H.P. Lovecraft.

"The Hound." First appeared in *Skull Comics* No. 4 (1972).

14. *H.P. Lovecraft's Cthulhu* No. 1 (December 1991). Millennium Comics.

"The Whisperer in Darkness," Part One. Edited by Paul Davis. Written by Terry Collins and Paul Davis. Pencils by Don Heck. Inks by Robert Lewis. Colors by Mark Menendez and Frank Turner. Art direction by Melissa Martin. Cover by Joe Phillips. The Miskatonic Project created by Mark Ellis.

This book includes two "trading cards" featuring depictions of Cthulhu and explaining the god's origins, and other information.

15. *H.P. Lovecraft's Cthulhu* No. 2 (March 1992). Millennium Comics.

"The Whisperer in Darkness," Part Two. Edited by Paul Davis. Written by Terry Collins and Paul Davis. Pencils by Don Heck. Inks by Robert Lewis. Colors by Mark Menendez and Frank Turner. Art direction by Melissa Martin. Cover by Joe Phillips. The Miskatonic Project created by Mark Ellis.

This book includes two 'trading cards" featuring depictions and explanations of Lovecraftian gods Hastur and M-Go.

16. *Lovecraft in Full Color* No. 1 (December 1991). Adventure Comics.

"The Lurking Fear." From the original short story by H.P. Lovecraft. Adapted by Steve Jones and Octavio Cariello. Lettered by Tim Eldred. Interior coloring by Katy Llewellyn. Cover painting by Jeff Remmer. Published by Dave Olbrich.

Each edition of this title contains an installment of "The History of Comic Books" by Jim Korkis.

17. *Lovecraft in Full Color* No. 2 (March 1992). Adventure Comics.

"Beyond the Wall of Sleep." From the original short story by H.P. Lovecraft. Adapted by Steve Jones and Octavio Cariello. Lettered by Tim Eldred. Interior coloring by Katy Llewellyn. Cover painting by Jeff Remmer. Published by Dave Olbrich.

18. *Lovecraft in Full Color* No. 3 (April, 1992). Adventure Comics.

"The Tomb." From the original short story by H.P. Lovecraft.

Adapted by Steve Jones and Octavio Cariello. Lettered by Tim Eldred. Interior coloring by Katy Llewellyn. Cover painting by Jeff Remmer. Published by Dave Olbrich.

19. *Lovecraft in Full Color* No. 4 (May 1992). Adventure Comics.

"The Alchemist." From the original short story by H.P. Lovecraft. Adapted by Steve Jones and Octavio Cariello. Lettered by Tim Eldred. Interior coloring by Katy Llewellyn. Cover by Jeff Remmer. Published by Dave Olbrich.

20. *The Worlds of H.P. Lovecraft: Dagon, Part One* (January 1993). Caliber Press. Black and white.

Adapted by Steven Philip Jones and Sergio Cariello, from a story by H.P. Lovecraft.

21. *The Worlds of H.P. Lovecraft: Dagon, Part Two* (February 1993). Caliber Press. Black and white.

Adapted by Steven Jones and Sergio Cariello, from a story by H.P. Lovecraft. Published by Gary Reed.

22. *The Worlds of H.P. Lovecraft: The Music of Erich Zann* (March 1993). Caliber Press. Black and white.

Adapted by Steven Philip Jones, from a story by H.P. Lovecraft. Illustrated and lettered by Aldin Baroza. Published by Gary Reed. Production by Nate Pride.

23. *The Worlds of H.P. Lovecraft: The Picture in the House* (April, 1993). Caliber Press. Black and white.

Adapted by Steven Philip Jones, from a story by H.P. Lovecraft. Illustrated by Rob Davis. Lettered by Susan Dorne. Published by Gary Reed. Production by Mark Winfrey and Nate Pride.

This book also includes a piece titled "Howard Phillips Lovecraft: How He Faced the Greatest Horror ... Death" by Steven Philip Jones. Jones notes that most of the information in his piece was gleaned from "Death of a Gentleman: The Last Days of Howard Phillips Lovecraft."

24. *The Worlds of H.P. Lovecraft: Dagon* (June and July 1993). Caliber Press. Black and white.

Artwork by Sergio Cariello.

25. *The Worlds of H.P. Lovecraft: Arthur Jermyn* (August 1993). Caliber Press. Black and white.

Adapted by Steven Philip Jones and Wayne Reid, from "Facts Concerning the Late Arthur Jermyn and His Family," by H.P. Lovecraft. Artwork by Wayne Reid.

26. *The Starry Wisdom* (1994). Creation Books.

"The Call of Cthulhu." Adapted by Ron Coulthart, from the story by H.P. Lovecraft.

27. *The Worlds of H.P. Lovecraft: The Statement of Randolph Carter* (1996). Caliber Press.

Adapted by Steven Philip Jones and Chris Jones, from the story by H.P. Lovecraft.

28. *The Worlds of H.P. Lovecraft: The Alchemist* (1997). Caliber Press.

First appeared in *Lovecraft in Full Color* No 4 (May 1992).

29. *The Worlds of H.P. Lovecraft: The Tomb* (1997). Caliber Press.

First appeared in *Lovecraft in Full Color* No. 3 (April 1992).

30. *The Worlds of H.P. Lovecraft: The Lurking Fear* (1997). Caliber Press.

First appeared in *Lovecraft in Full Color* No. 1 (December 1991).

31. *The Worlds of H.P. Lovecraft: Beyond the Wall of Sleep* (1998). Caliber Press.

First appeared in *Lovecraft in Full Color* No. 2 (March 1992).

32. *H.P. Lovecraft's The Dream Quest of Unknown Kadath* Nos. 1–5 (November 1997 to February 1999).

Adapted by Jason Thompson, from the novella by H.P. Lovecraft.

33. *The Haunter of the Dark and Other Grotesque Visions* (2000). Oneiros Books. Black and white.

"The Call of Cthulhu." First appeared in *The Starry Wisdom* (1994). Creation Books.

"The Haunter of the Dark." Adapted by John Coulthart, from the story by H.P. Lovecraft.

"The Dunwich Horror." Adapted by John Coulthart, from the story by H.P. Lovecraft.

34. *Graphics Classics: H.P. Lovecraft* Volume 4 (2002). Eureka Productions. Black and white.

Designed and published by Tom Pomplun. Editorial assistant, Eileen Fitzgerald. Introduction by Gahan Wilson.

"H.P. Lovecraft 1890–1937." By George Kuchar. Originally appeared in *Arcade* No. 3 (1975).

"Herbert West: Renanimator." Illustrated by Richard Corben, Rick Geary, J.B. Bonivert, and Mark A. Nelson. Frontispiece by R.K. Sloane. Story by H.P. Lovecraft, edited and abridged by Tom Pomplum (2002).

"The Dream-Quest of Unknown Kadath." A portfolio based on the H.P. Lovecraft novel. Illustrated by Tom Sutton. Originally appeared in a limited edition portfolio from Another World, Ltd. (1978).

"The Outsider." Illustrated by Devon Devereaux. Story by H.P. Lovecraft, edited and abridged by Tom Pomplum (2002).

"The Shadow out of Time." Adapted and illustrated by Matt Howsarth. Story by H.P. Lovecraft (2002).

"In a Sequester'd Providence Churchyard Where Once Poe Walk'd." By H.P. Lovecraft. Art by Dierdre Luzwick (2002).

"The Terrible Old Man." Illustrated by Onsmith Jeremi. Story by H.P. Lovecraft.

"The Cats of Ulthar." Illustrated by Lisa K. Weber. Story by H.P. Lovecraft, edited and abridged by Tom Pomplum (2002).

"Cthulhu's Dreams: Le Chaos Râpant." Written and illustrated by Dominique Signoret. Originally appeared in French in *Sens Fiction* (1999). Revised and reprinted by permission of the artist.

"Fungi from Yuggoth." Poem by H.P. Lovecraft. Illustrated by Stephen Hickman, John Coulthart, Maxon Crumb, Kellie Strom, Allen Koszowski, S. Clay Wilson, Skot Olsen, Jeffrey Johannes, Steven Cerio,

Gerry Alanguilan, Peter Von Sholly, Arnold Arre, Andy Ewen, Rafael Avila, Jeff Remmer, Trina Robbins and R.K. Sloane.

"Reflections from R'Lyeh." Written and illustrated by Chris Pelletiere.

"About the Artists and Writers." Illustrated by Allen Koszowski. Cover illustration by Todd Schorr, back cover illustration by Jeff Remmer. Additional illustrations by Saverio Tenuta, Jim Nelson, Paul Carrick, and Giorgio Comolo.

35. *Lovecraft* (2003). DC.

Written by Hans Rodionoff and Keith Giffen. Artwork and coloring by Enrique Breccia.

This Lovecraft comic is a bit different, as it is a depiction of Lovecraft's life. As an ad proclaims: "From his bizarre childhood through his adult days Lovecraft was haunted by grotesque visions. He dedicated his life to writing blood-boiling 'fictional' tales all in an attempt to appease his living nightmares. But that obsession would take its toll. Lovecraft would spend most of his life as a recluse, his only company being his demons and the occasional visit to his publisher. The story of America's greatest horror writer is a tale as haunting as the demons that plagued him." Anyone familiar with Lovecraft knows what a pile of manure this is. Yes, Lovecraft had his demons (as most of us do), but to imply that the author wrote from direct life experience is absurd. Still, the comic is interesting and well done.

It is appropriate that the first Lovecraft adaptations appeared in EC Comics, which were to comic books what *Weird Tales* was to the pulps. These comics came under fire from Dr. Frederick Wertham's damning of comic book sex and violence in his extremely influential book *The Seduction of the Innocent* (1954). In the book, Wertham built a case that many morally subversive comic books were drugs designed to addict the young to unhealthy thoughts. Comics, he asserted, were leading innocent children into depression, depravity, and lives of violence; and children were copying the grotesque acts depicted in the comic books of the day and becoming juvenile delinquents.

Wertham's crusade led to Senate hearings and to the creation of the formation of the Comics Magazine Association of America Inc., an organization of comic book publishers devoted to self-regulation of their products. These occurrences ended EC Comics' "reign of terror."

Lovecraft did not appear in the comic book medium again until 1969. Beginning with its fourth issue, *Skull Comics* began devoting itself to Lovecraft adaptations. And why not? The public was becoming reacquainted with Lovecraft via a series of paperback collections of his work.

Finally, in 1992, *Adventure Comics* published a tie-in for the movie *Re-Animator*, as well as a prequel. The tie-in, however, is more an adaptation of the film than of Lovecraft's story.

PART SEVEN

Music Inspired by Lovecraft

H.P. Lovecraft, the Band: 1967–1969

Chicago has always been a city of eclectic music with roots in the blues, jazz, folk, and rock. In 1967, however, five talented musicians with varying musical backgrounds came together to produce a mix of jazz, folk, rock, and psychedelia that could only have arisen in the late sixties.

Guitarist George Edwards was a folk singer in the early sixties who turned to rock in the middle of the decade to cut a single on Chicago's Dunwich label. The record's A-side covered the Beatles' "Norwegian Wood," and the B-side covered Bob Dylan's "Quit Your Lowdown Ways" and featured Steve Miller on guitar. The record was not released until the early seventies, but by that time, the band H.P. Lovecraft had come and gone. Edwards also sang backup on several hits by the Shadows of Night, a Chicago band with national appeal. By late 1966, however, Edwards was part of a jazz trio playing local Holiday Inns. In that band was classically trained singer and keyboardist Dave Michaels. These two formed the nucleus of the band they called H.P. Lovecraft. Their first release was "Anyway That You Want Me/It's All Over for You," the latter a solo effort by Edwards and an obvious rip-off of Bob Dylan's "It's All Over Now, Baby Blue."

Soon to join Edwards and Michaels were guitarist Tony Cavalleri, drummer Michael Tegza, and Shadows of Night rhythm guitarist Jerry

McGeorge. Although personnel would change from 1967 to 1969, these five were the H.P. Lovecraft responsible for the band's studio recordings and unique sound.

The group's first album, produced by Dunwich, was the self-titled *H.P. Lovecraft* (PHS 600–252), released by Phillips Records in 1967. The cover features the band members on stone steps on the right with the rest of the cover devoted to the leaves of a climbing plant. The cover is black and white except for psychedelic shapes and colors superimposed on half of the leaves. The cover suggests something extraordinary in the midst of normality, just what one would expect from a band named after H.P. Lovecraft. Liner notes include the following:

> All we want is to be able to do our own thing. It's not easy to do — for some, next to impossible, but H.P. Lovecraft struggles on." — George Edwards

> Everything has changed in the months since George, David, Jerry, Mike, and Tony arrived; individually at different times, from different environments and musical bags, and found each other with different people, at different places.

> All of this would just naturally lead one to believe that the group (H.P. Lovecraft) had to be different. It is!

As one might expect, the liner notes also provide some information on author H.P. Lovecraft:

> H.P. Lovecraft, novelist and poet, died March 15th, 1937, of cancer and Bright's Disease in Providence, Rhode Island.
> Born August 20th, 1890, Lovecraft was always susceptible to the cold, not being able to tolerate temperatures below 30.
> Lovecraft was best known for his macabre tales and poems of Earth populated by another race. According to Lovecraft's legend, this race with its own gods and religion was expelled from Earth for practicing black magic. However, they remained on the periphery of human life, practicing their nether rites and waiting for an opportunity to repossess Earth.
> "Fungi of Yuggoth" is thought by many to be his finest poem. "The Dunwich Horror" is one of his most popular novels. Following his death, Lovecraft was laid to rest in his Grandfather's plot in Swan Point Cemetery.
> — Ethan Reusin

Album credits are as follows:

> George Edwards: Guitar & Bass (Amplified 6-String/Acoustic 6-String, Acoustic 12-String and Guitaroon), Vocals.
> Dave Michaels: Organ, Harpsichord, Piano, Clarinet, Recorder, Vocals.
> Tony Cavalleri: Lead Guitar, Vocals.
> Jerry McGeorge: Bass, Vocals.
> Michael Tegza: Drums, Tympani & Assorted Percussion, Vocals.
> Orchestra: Len Druss — Clarinet, Piccolo, English Horn, Bass and Tenor Saxophones. Paul Tervelt — French Horn. Jack Henningbaum — French Horn. Ralph Craig — Trombone. Herb Weiss — Trombone. Clyde Bachand — Tuba. Bill Traub — Reeds. Eddie Higgins — Vibes. Bill Traut — Bell (1811 Ship's Bell).
> All tunes arranged by H.P. Lovecraft — Horns arranged by Eddie Higgins.

At the end of the notes, Dunwich Productions Inc. gratefully acknowledged the cooperation of the H.P. Lovecraft Estate, August Derleth and Arkham House Publishing for the use of the group's name and titles from Lovecraft's work. The notes suggested listeners write to Arkham House in Sauk City, Wisconsin, for more information concerning author Lovecraft.

The album contains ten cuts:

Side One

1. "Wayfaring Stranger" (G. Edwards), Yuggoth Music Co. (BMI), 2:35.

The first cut introduces the album's main themes of travel and movement. Lovecraft's fiction frequently addresses those themes in the form of travel from one dimension to another as part of understanding the true and generally horrible nature of our universe. The song is ultimately upbeat, however, as the stranger looks forward to "going home" to be with his brothers. The reference is, of course, to death and the hope for an afterlife. Contrary to anything Lovecraftian, the song has appeared in many church hymnals.

2. "Let's Get Together" (C. Powers), S.F.O. Music, Inc. (BMI), 4:35.

This song was originally released by the California pop quintet We Five in August 1965, but survived on the charts only two weeks, rising only as high as number 31. H.P. Lovecraft's version, featuring driving vocals with rolling organ notes, is superior. The song reached its greatest popularity when the Youngbloods released it in August 1969 and it became an anthem of the young generation, climbing to number 5 on the charts during its 12-week run. The upbeat song was, again in an un–Lovecraftian way, repopularized as the theme for the National Council of Christians and Jews.

3. "I've Been Wrong Before" (R. Newman), January Music (BMI), 2:46.

This song, written by then-little-known Randy Newman, slows down the album's pace with haunting instrumental backup and lyrics of betrayed love. The song had already been a hit in Great Britain for Cilla Black.

4. "The Drifter" (T. Edmundson), Carte Music (BMI), 4.11.

This song returns to the theme of travel and movement.

5. "That's the Bag I'm In" (F. Neil), Coconut Grove (BMI), 1:46.

This song from Fred Neil's debut album is highlighted by the harmonies of Edwards and Michaels. The lyrics explain the plight of an individual for whom everything in life goes wrong.

Side Two

1. "The White Ship" (Edwards, Michaels, Cavallari), Yuggoth Music Co. (BMI), 6:37.

"The White Ship," adapted from Lovecraft's story of the same name, is simply one of the most haunting songs ever recorded. It is the best cut ever laid down by H.P. Lovecraft, and it alone is worth the price of admission. Exotic sounds from a variety of instruments are augmented by the haunting sound of an 1811 ship's bell "played" by Bill Traut. The overall effect could not be better.

The singer laments that he cannot go all the way to his dream world on the White Ship. Still he waits. The instrumental interlude is positively transcendental.

2. "Country Boy & Bleecker Street" (F. Neil), Coconut Grove (BMI), 2:35.

Songwriter and singer Fred Neil makes his second contribution to the album with this rocking lament of a country boy who is spiritually lost in the big city and just wants to go home. As such, it fits in with the album's overall theme of travel and of being lost in environments one does not understand.

3. "The Time Machine" (G. Edwards, D. Michaels), Yuggoth Music Co. (BMI), 2:05.

"The Time Machine" is a light-hearted entry with a sound reminiscent of the New Vaudeville Band's hit "Winchester Cathedral." The piece doesn't really fit the mood of the rest of the album. Except for its obvious reference to a journey, the song takes us further from the mood of H.P. Lovecraft and indeed from the band's own strengths.

4. "That's How Much I Love You, Baby (More or Less)" (G. Edwards, D. Michaels, T. Cavallari), Yuggoth Music Co. (BMI), 3:55.

This song returns to the album's dominant mood. It is a dreamy, laid-back lament about the girl who has left her man and gone to L.A. for a better, faster life. That was how much she loved him, more or less.

5. "Gloria Patria" (Traditional), Yuggoth Music Co. (BMI), :26.

This short piece is the "Gloria Patria" of Roman Catholic tradition. Why it is the final piece on this album, or is on this album at all, is a mystery. It contends against the overall mood of the album and is very un–Lovecraftian.

H.P. Lovecraft's second and last studio album was titled simply *H.P. Lovecraft II.* In the meantime Jeff Boyan had replaced McGeorge, and the group was opening for such acts as Donovan, Pink Floyd, Procol Harum, Jefferson Airplane, Buffalo Springfield, and Big Brother and the Holding Company. To be precise, the name of H.P. Lovecraft had been enmeshed with the psychedelic phenomenon of the late sixties. As a result, augmented by ever-deeper drug experimentation, the group produced music increasingly based on Lovecraftian reality distortion. The results on the second album were mixed.

Side One

1. "Spin, Spin, Spin" (Callier)

The album begins well with a melodic daydream. The music induces a mood of sweet reverie.

2. "It's About Time" (Callier)

This song might have worked in the late sixties, but it is now dreadfully dated. A psychedelic version of "We Shall Overcome," it expresses the late sixties' and early seventies' hope for a better world, but it draws its life and style from that time and does not hold up well today.

3. "Blue Jack of Diamonds" (Boyan)

This is a haunting ballad in tune with what H.P. Lovecraft (the band) should have been doing. A bell rings, reminiscent of "The White Ship." But this is a bell ringing the hour and signaling that all is well for the blue jack of diamonds. But is it? The point is that time and love do not always coincide. The queen leaves the king of hearts. Should we love the one we have or love the one we want? Left behind, the king of hearts becomes the blue jack of diamonds.

4. "Electrollentando" (Edwards)

"Twirling, twirling, swirling" and off we go into a psychedelic tune that is today nearly unlistenable unless one is totally stoned.

Side Two

1. "At the Mountains of Madness" (Cavallari/Edwards/Michaels)

Here we return to Lovecraft big-time. To a driving beat, H.P. Lovecraft transports us to a musically conjured brink of madness. The organ is unnerving and the vocals irresistible. The song ends with a soft, mad laugh. Very appropriate.

2. "Mobius Trip" (Edwards)

This is another of those few songs that the group should not have recorded. Trying to depict a psychedelic experience, the song only succeeds in dating itself and being embarrassing.

3. "High Flying Bird" (Wheeler)

This song, already covered by Jefferson Airplane and Judy Henske, is one of the high points of the album. It is a welcome folk rock respite from the band's dated psychedelia.

4. "Nothing's Boy" (Nordine)

Here we have a strange cut. Not bad, just strange. "Radio word-jazzmeister" Ken Nordine wrote and provides the spoken words for this psychedelic interlude.

5. "The Keeper of the Keys" (Brewer/Shipley)

This song, written by recording artists Brewer and Shipley, is a mystery to critics. Is the vocal simply over-reaching opera, or is it parody? Despite the critics, the piece is enjoyable.

Long after the demise of H.P. Lovecraft as a group, a live album was issued from a May 11, 1968, concert. And a fine album it is. The cuts are:

1. "Wayfaring Stranger"
2. "The Drifter"
3. "It's About Time"
4. "The White Ship"
5. "At the Mountains of Madness"
6. "The Bad I'm In"
7. "I've Been Wrong Before"
8. "Country Boy & Bleecker Street"

Again, the high point is "The White Ship." Significantly, the group H.P. Lovecraft also demonstrates that it can produce its studio sound in concert, something many groups of that time could not easily do.

For the best musical experience, listen to the live album as it is, but make a compilation tape or burn a CD of the following songs from the two studio albums:

Side One

1. "Wayfaring Stranger"
2. "Let's Get Together"

3. "I've Been Wrong Before"
4. "The Drifter"
5. "That's the Bag I'm In"
6. "The White Ship"

Side Two
1. "Country Boy and Bleecker Street"
2. "That's How Much I Love You, Baby"
3. "Spin, Spin, Spin"
4. "Blue Jack of Diamonds"
5. "At the Mountains of Madness"
6. "High Flying Bird"
7. "Keeper of the Keys"

The Beatles should have chosen their best cuts from the three-record *White Album* and produced one great classic one- or two-record album. Similarly, H.P. Lovecraft could have created one great album had they combined the best of their first two albums into one product. This was a very talented musical group. Apparently, their fame is greater in Europe today than it is in the U. S. Had they not tipped over into drug reveries, we might recognize them today as one of the great musical groups of their period.

After the group broke up in 1969, Edwards and Tegza re-formed in 1970 as Lovecraft (without the "H.P."). Before that group's album was released, however, Edwards was gone. The resulting album had little resemblance to the H.P. Lovecraft of a few years earlier.

Other Bands and Albums Inspired by Lovecraft

Too many bands to mention have recorded music reputedly inspired by H.P. Lovecraft, the writer. Most of these bands recorded in the 1990s as heavy metal and death metal bands, and most are unavailable from major Internet sellers. Listed below are a few of the bands and albums gleaned from www.hplovecraft.com most obviously inspired in some strange way by Lovecraft. The name of the band is followed by the band's key Lovecraftian album or albums.

1. Necronomicon: *The Silver Key* (1996); *Pharaoh of Gods* (1999).

2. Not Breathing: *A Fire in the Bronx Zoo* (1997); *The Starry Wisdom* (1998).

3. Rage: *Black in Mind* (1995).

4. Rudimentary Peni: *Cacophany* (1989).

PART EIGHT

Roleplaying Lovecraft

There are several games inspired by Lovecraft's writings, but for my money, the best one is *Call of Cthulhu*, a roleplaying game by Sandy Peterson and Lynn Willis (Chaosium Inc., 1981, 1999, and 2001). At the time of its publication, three prestigious national awards were given for excellence in game design, and *Call of Cthulhu* won all three. Because Lovecraft is popular worldwide, foreign language editions of the game were issued in Finnish, French, German, Hungarian, Italian, Japanese, Polish, and Spanish. In 1996, the game was chosen for the Origins Hall of Fame, gaming's most prestigious award.

Sandy Petersen writes in the foreword to the game book:

> My introduction to H.P. Lovecraft was as a child, when I found a tattered book of stories, printed for the use of servicemen during World War II. I read that book in bed that night, and become [sic] entranced forever. If you, too, love Lovecraft's stories, you can now experience the Cthulhu Mythos in a new way. What would you have done in the place of Lovecraft's intrepid heroes? Could you have solved the sinister Whateley mystery? Would you have been able to save the world from the nightmare of the deep ones? Could you face shoggoths without going mad? Now you can find out!

And indeed you can. The game book begins with a printing of Lovecraft's story "The Call of Cthulhu." The introduction then gives some background on Lovecraft himself and explains his place in popular culture. In the process, we are told that "now he is generally recognized as the major American horror-story writer of the twentieth century."

The introduction continues with the rules of the game. First there are the characters of the investigators, who attempt to solve the mystery. Another character, the Keeper of Arcane Lore,

> chooses the scenario or creates the plot, sets the stage, describes the scene, portrays the people whom the investigators meet, and helps resolve the action.... Play is mostly talking: some situation or encounter is outlined, and then the players tell the keeper what they, in the guise of their investigators, intend to do. Using the rules to keep matters consistent and fair, the keeper then tells them if they can do what they proposed, and the steps they must follow. If the proposal is impossible, the keeper narrates what happens instead. Roll dice to resolve encounters. Dice keep everybody honest, add drama, and promote surprises, dismal defeats, and hair's-breadth escapes.

This is a very nuanced game, and there are many Lovecraftian words and names to master. It is even possible, in the context of the game, for investigators to go partially or completely insane. Many variations can occur, and the events and outcomes of no two games will be the same. The game book also lists many resources for play, including books and websites.

Those playing as investigators can create their characters, their occupations, their strength, constitution, size, intelligence, and other characteristics, all of which personalizes the game. There are rules for using firearms and other types of weapons. As I said before, the Mythos can cause insanity; various therapies are available for treatment.

The game involves encounters with many occult books drawn from Lovecraft and his circle. Sorcerers can cast spells, and it is good to know one's way through such arcane matters.

The game book continues with references:

1. The Cthulhu Mythos
2. *The Necronomicon*
3. Howard Phillips Lovecraft
4. In Rerum Supernatura

5. Mental Disorders
6. Keeper's Lore
7. Creatures of the Mythos
8. Alien Technology
9. Deities of the Mythos
10. Beasts and Monsters
11. Personalities
12. A Mythos Grimoire

The game book then lays out several scenarios:

1. The Haunting
2. Edge of Darkness
3. The Madman
4. Dead Man Stomp

These scenarios are, of course, inspired by Lovecraft's stories. I should mention that a game takes at least an evening to play, but the rewards are ample.

The game book provides a guide to Lovecraft country, including a map, optional rules involving vehicle chases, a list of 1890s costs for equipment and services as opposed to present day costs, references for keepers and players, a list of natural and man-made disasters, criminal and futurist occult events, and a historical timeline.

The game book includes a "comic book" drawn by Tim Callender which begins: "Call of Cthulhu is the only role-playing game where ... the gamemaster says 'you see a large cave ahead,' and the characters respond with, 'I think my mother's calling me.'" Finally, the game book provides several pages of play aids.

The publishers also provide two additional books to help improve one's play: *The 1920s Investigator Companion* and *The Creature Companion*.

The Call of Cthulhu presently carries a price of $37.95, and it is worth every penny. Both Lovecraft aficionados and those unfamiliar with the author can enjoy this game, but obviously the more one knows, the more one will enjoy. There is enough here to provide players a lifetime of entertainment. As the back cover says: "To play all you need are this book, some dice, and your friends."

PART NINE

The Lovecraft Legacy

Lovecraft's fiction comprises three general types:

1. Gothic stories influenced largely by Edgar Allan Poe, M.R. James, Algernon Blackwood, and Arthur Machen.
2. Dream stories influenced by Lord Dunsany.
3. The Cthulhu Mythos, a synthesis of horror and science-fantasy fiction unique to Lovecraft.

First we will briefly review the status of other authors in the weird fiction genre and attempt to assign Lovecraft his proper place among them. Any evaluation of this kind is, of course, subjective.

1. Mary Shelley (1797–1851) contributed several works to the horror–science fiction genre, but her lasting contribution will always remain the novel *Frankenstein*. That novel has been adapted countless times in the cinema and has contributed no small amount to the comic book industry and radio. Few can compete with Mrs. Shelley when it comes to influence on popular culture, but her reputation rests mainly on one work. Lovecraft and others have produced more works of popular influence than Shelley. So, for producing one work of permanent influence, Shelley reigns, but for producing a large body of work that has influenced popular culture, many other writers eclipse her. Shelley's genre work is philosophical in nature, as both *Frankenstein* and *The Last Man* attest, but so is Lovecraft's best work. Lovecraft would scorn Shelley's withdrawal from Percy's atheism and her later years of conventional thinking. Lovecraft lived his vision to the end, and although Shelley wrote one book of lasting power, Lovecraft challenges her in the field of popular culture due to his greater productivity.

2. Nathaniel Hawthorne (1804–1864) is one of the greatest nineteenth century American writers. Although Lovecraft disliked Hawthorne's tendency toward allegory, the latter's tales of guilt and ambiguity are a fearful introduction to the dark side of Puritan life, to American life, and to the human condition in general. Poe praised Hawthorne highly, as he should have. Five of Hawthorne's best weird tales are "Young Goodman Brown," "The Minister's Black Veil," "Rappaccini's Daughter," "Feathertop" and "The Birthmark," the first three of which are superior to Lovecraft's best. Still, Lovecraft is far ahead of Hawthorne in his influence on popular culture. In 1963, Hollywood cast Vincent Price in *Twice-Told Tales*, an omnibus featuring adaptations of Hawthorne's "Dr. Heidegger's Experiment," "Rappaccini's Daughter," and *The House of the Seven Gables*. It was a fine film, but it didn't do as well as the Poe films circulating at that time. Therefore, the idea of further Hawthorne films was abandoned.

3. Edgar A. Poe (1809–1845) exerted a strong influence on Lovecraft, as he has on most weird fiction authors after 1845. On the positive side, Poe invented the detective story, teased readers with science fiction so realistic that many confused it with fact, conjured ethereal fantasies, and spun tales and poems of beauty and terror. However, major literary critics such as D.H. Lawrence and Harold Bloom have found much of his work puerile. Lovecraft's writings have also been attacked by top critics for the same failing. While, that charge can be made of some of the works of both writers, the blanket charge is not sustainable. Anyway, Lovecraft openly wrote of his debt to Poe, and many of his earlier stories are clearly Poesque in tone and theme. Poe's gothic tales are superior to Lovecraft's, however, because Poe is both technically and psychologically superior. With the possible exceptions of Robert Bloch, Colin Wilson, and Ramsey Campbell, Poe is able to examine the terrifying depths of a deranged mind better than any other writer of weird fiction. Poe's five best tales, arguably, are "The Fall of the House of Usher," "The Black Cat," "The Masque of the Red Death," "The Tell-Tale Heart," and "The Man of the Crowd," all of which are superior to Lovecraft's best stories. Thus far, Poe and his work have contributed more to popular culture than any other writer of weird fiction.

4. Sheridan Le Fanu (1814–1873) was ahead of his time in that his weird fiction plumbed psychological depths previously left unexplored. In many ways, Le Fanu's best work is superior to Lovecraft's. Five of Le Fanu's best weird fiction tales are "Green Tea," "The Haunted Baronet," "Schalken the Painter," "Madame Crowl's Ghost," and, of course, the novella *Carmilla*. Except for a handful of films based on *Carmilla*, Le Fanu's influence on popular culture is minimal. Today, Lovecraft is much better known by the public than Le Fanu.

5. Ambrose Bierce (1842–1914). Although Bierce has earned Poe's mantle for creating frightening stories of guilt and troubled human psychology, little of his work has been adapted to popular culture venues. Some of his most effective stories are "The Death of Halpin Frayser," "The Damned Thing," "An Occurrence at Owl Creek Bridge," "A Tough Tussle," "The Moonlit Road," and "The Eyes of the Panther." The most memorable Bierce contribution to film and television remains the French short subject "An Occurrence at Owl Creek Bridge" (1961) directed by Robert Enrico and turned into a *Twilight Zone* episode telecast on February 28, 1964. Other films based on Bierce's work are *The Man and the Snake* (1972), *The Return* (1973) and *The Eyes of the Panther* (1989). At this point, Lovecraft towers over Bierce as an overall contributor to popular culture.

6. Bram Stoker (1847–1912) is best known as the author of *Dracula*. Most of his weird short stories are collected in *Dracula's Guest and Other Weird Stories*. Five of Stoker's best weird fiction tales are "Dracula's Guest," "The Judge's House" (which may have influenced Lovecraft's "Dreams in the Witch House"), "The Burial of the Rats," "A Dream of Red Hands," and "The Coming of Abel Behenna." Of these, only "The Judge's House" is a good story, and Lovecraft's best weird stories eclipse Stoker's by miles. Stoker remains a popular cultural icon primarily due to *Dracula.* Ken Russell directed a very good adaptation of Stoker's *The Lair of the White Worm,* and there have been several mediocre adaptations of his *Jewel of Seven Stars.* Today, Stoker probably outdistances Lovecraft in the field of popular culture largely due to *Dracula.*

7. Robert Louis Stevenson (1850–1894) is one of the greatest writers of weird fiction to come along, due to his technical skill and psychological insight. Five of Stevenson's most effective weird fiction tales are "The Body Snatcher," "Thrawn Janet," "Markheim," "The Bottle Imp," and of course, the novella *The Strange Case of Dr. Jekyll and Mr. Hyde.* When Stevenson turned to weird fiction, his best work is technically far superior to Lovecraft's. Lovecraft, however, rivals Stevenson in the realm of popular culture. Stevenson's *Dr. Jekyll and Mr. Hyde* has been presented as stage plays, movies, television episodes, and comic books, but the only other Stevenson weird fiction tales adapted to film have been "The Body Snatcher" and "The Sire de Maletroit's Door" (as *The Strange Door,* 1951). In the latter case, the story itself was not actually weird fiction, but it was made into a "horror film" starring Charles Laughton and Boris Karloff. *Dr. Jekyll and Mr. Hyde* and "The Bottle Imp" were adapted as *Classics Illustrated* comic books. "Markeim" was adapted to television in 1952, 1974, and 1990.

Stevenson will undoubtedly survive with afficionados of great fiction, but except for *Dr. Jekyll and Mr. Hyde* and "The Body Snatcher," he has not had much effect on popular culture as a weird fiction writer.

8. Arthur Machen (1863–1947), inspired by Irish legends, spoke of terrors too horrible for human beings to know. Lovecraft took up that theme in his own writing. Three of Machen's best stories are "The Great God Pan," "Novel of the Black Seal," and "Novel of the White Powder." Lovecraft is equal, if not superior, to Machen. Popular culture has certainly turned to Lovecraft much more than it has to Machen. Research for this book did not reveal a single Machen adaptation

9. Algernon Blackwood (1869–1951) wrote some of the greatest horror and supernatural tales in the English language. Influenced by psychology and mysticism, he wrote of elemental pantheistic powers that menace humankind. Some excellent examples are "Ancient

Sorceries," "The Glamour of the Snow," "The Other Wing," "The Wendigo," and "The Willows," most of which are superior to anything Lovecraft wrote. Nevertheless, Lovecraft has had more of his work adapted to popular culture venues than has Blackwood.

Perhaps the most memorable Blackwood television adaptation is that of "The Wendigo" on *Great Ghost Stories* (1961), one scene of which had the terrifying and memorable cry, "Oh, my flaming feet of fire." Other Blackwood television adaptations include, "The Listener" on *Mystery and Imagination* (1968) and "The Doll" on *Night Gallery* (1971). *Wendigo* appeared as a film in 1978.

10. Lord Dunsany (1878–1957) strongly influenced Lovecraft's dream stories. Lovecraft's fantasies shared with Dunsany's an aversion to the materialism seen in such books as *The Sword of Welleran and Other Stories* (1908), and his Cthulhu Mythos exhibits the influence of such Dunsany works as *The Gods of Pegana* (1905) and *Time and the Gods* (1906). A brief sampling of Dunsany's works suggests that Lovecraft was Dunsay's equal in the ability to create "word music." Unfortunately, Dunsany is largely unread today, and Lovecraft's shadow eclipses him almost totally in the realm of popular culture.

11. Robert E. Howard (1906–1936), a prolific *Weird Tales* contributor, is best known today as the creator of Conan the Barbarian, a character who has found his way into both films and comic books. His most eerie tale, however, is undoubtedly "Pigeons from Hell," which *Thriller* featured as one of the most terrifying television experiences of all time. His other stories are best known today via hardback and paperback anthologies. Howard, who regularly corresponded with Lovecraft, committed suicide after the death of his mother. Although Howard wrote exciting, if not always masterful, tales in a variety of genres (horror, Western, Oriental, sword and sorcery, and mystery), his place in popular culture, while significant, has not approached that of Lovecraft, who liked to refer to him as "Two-Gun Bob."

12. Shirley Jackson (1916–1965) wrote what is possibly the most terrifying short story of the modern era — "The Lottery," which was recently adapted as a made-for-television movie. Jackson's *The Haunt-*

ing of Hill House was twice filmed as *The Haunting* (1963 and 1999). Another of her books, *A Bird's Nest*, was filmed in 1957 as *Lizzie*. Many of her other short stories are horrific and psychologically disturbing. Unfortunately, she has been little adapted into popular culture beyond a few films and teleplays.

13. Robert Bloch (1917–1994) was a Lovecraft disciple and correspondent who went on to carve out his own niche in the horror pantheon during Lovecraft's life and after his death in 1937. Without reading the entirety of Bloch's work (he was incredibly prolific), many superior stories can still be picked out, such as "The Gloating Place," "Yours Truly, Jack the Ripper," "Enoch," "Lizzie Borden Took an Axe," "The Skull of the Marquis de Sade," and of course, the novel *Psycho*. Although Lovecraft's fiction taps more cosmic aspects than does Bloch's, Bloch has clearly had the greater impact on popular culture. His teleplays and screenplays alone have lifted him into realms of the top popular-culture horror authors of his generation. Among his stories adapted for television, ten were adapted by *Alfred Hitchcock Presents*, one by *Bus Stop*, six by *The Alfred Hitchcock Hour*, three by *Star Trek*, and two by *Journey to the Unknown*. His stories have also often been adapted in comic book format.

14. Richard Matheson (b. 1926) has had a powerful influence on popular culture by way of the pulps, teleplays, screenplays, comic book adaptations, films, and television shows. He is best known for his novels *The Shrinking Man*, *I Am Legend*, and *Hell House*, all of which were adapted to the big screen. As Matheson wrote, "the leitmotif of all my work ... is as follows: *The individual isolated in a threatening world, attempting to survive.*"* Few approaches to fiction capture the human condition and horror better than that. A few of Matheson's best short stories are "Long Distance Call," "Dance of the Dead," "Legion of Plotters," "The Distributor," and "Duel." Lovecraft's best work is more cosmic in its horror, but Matheson's work delivers a chill equal to Lovecraft. In addition, Matheson's impact on popular culture surpasses that of Lovecraft.

*Bloom, Harold, ed. *Modern Horror Writers*. New York: Chelsea House, 1995.

15. Stephen King (b. 1947) is undoubtedly the greatest pop culture horror icon of all time. He has done everything from writing novels, short stories, screenplays, and teleplays to directing a film and appearing in film adaptations of his own work. He has written a book-length critique of modern literary and cinematic horror works, and his work has been adapted by every medium possible. Some of King's most effective works are his novels *The Shining, Salem's Lot, The Dead Zone, The Dark Tower: The Gunslinger,* and *It.* King's later works are much less satisfying, although many of them, such as *Cujo* and *Needful Things,* can pull their weight. *Gerald's Game* is the low point of King's career. But, as today's young folks would say, "King rules!" His greatest strength is the ability to include myriads of popular culture references in his tales, which lull the reader with familiarity and comfort before the unleashing of some extraordinary horror. All considered, King is a greater player in the realm of popular culture than Lovecraft.

We must remember that Howard, Bloch, King, and many others are the popular culture icons that they are at least in part because of Lovecraft's direct influence. Now the evaluation process changes somewhat. Lovecraft's reputation as a popular culture icon is growing, but it still falls behind some of the modern and contemporary reputations. A recent publication, *Eternal Lovecraft: The Persistence of HPL in Popular Culture* (1998), edited by Jim Turner, features such Lovecraft-inspired stories as "Sensible City" by Harlan Ellison, "Ralph Wollstonecraft Hedge: A Memoir" by Ron Goulart, "Crouch End" by Stephen King, "The Other Dead Man" by Gene Wolfe, "The Events of Poroth Farm" by T.E.D. Klein," and "A Bit of the Dark World" by Fritz Leiber.

We can see from these examples that although many popular writers who have emerged after the death of H.P. Lovecraft have surpassed him in sheer numbers of film, teleplay, and comic book adaptations, these individuals draw their inspiration, at least in part, from Lovecraft. Lovecraft did not live in a time of mass culture such as many of our greatest genre authors do today, and he never had the outlets that are available to these new writers who have built on his foundation.

So where does H.P. Lovecraft stand today among the genre giants as far as popular culture visibility is concerned? If we rank all the genre masters considered in this chapter on a scale of 1 (lowest) to 10 (highest), Poe, Bloch, and King are obvious tens.

Shelley, Stevenson, Stoker, and Matheson are obvious nines.

Lovecraft is a seven, as is Shirley Jackson. Robert E. Howard and Hawthorne are probably a 6 (maybe a 7). Although writers such as Machen, Le Fanu, Blackwood and Bierce may be better writers than many named above, their influence on popular culture has not been as great. Dunsany is largely unadapted by popular culture.

There are, of course, other very good to great writers in the horror genre: Robert Aikman, E.F. Benson, Walter de la Mare, L.P. Hartley, M.R. James, and Fritz Leiber, among others. However, none of these have influenced popular culture as much as those named above. Leiber probably has the strongest claim as a challenger.

So, what will Lovecraft's legacy be with the passage of time? It may be that all writers will suffer as America moves into what must be feared as a post-literate age. Fewer people read regularly or seriously than ever before. But while Lovecraft may be read less as time goes on, his reputation may be enhanced by possible political and social movements of our day.

Today, America is polarized along political, cultural, racial, economic and secular-vs.-religious lines. No other genre writer so acutely experienced these polarities within his own life as Lovecraft did. Lovecraft admired the artistic and social legacy of pre–Enlightenment Western culture while detesting its tendency to supernatural worldviews. On the other hand, he admired the rationalism of the Enlightenment while detesting its tendencies toward democracy and egalitarianism.

Lovecraft's years in multiracial, multiethnic New York made him protective of the culture he loved and saw as being challenged and diluted by the Trojan horse of immigration.

As a well-read, creative rationalist, Lovecraft considered himself part of America's cultural elite. As he expressed in a letter:

> Equality is a joke — but a great abbey or cathedral, covered with moss, is a poignant reality. It is for us to safeguard and preserve the conditions which produce great abbeys, and palaces, and picturesque walled towns, and vivid sky-lines of steeples and domes, and luxurious tapestries and fascinating books, paintings, and statuary, and colossal organs and noble

music, and dramatic deeds on embattled fields.... *These are all
there is of life*; take them away and we have nothing which a
man of taste or spirit would care to live for. Take them away
and our poets have nothing to sing — our dreamers have nothing to dream about. The blood of a million men is well shed in
producing one glorious legend which thrills posterity ... and it
is not at all important *why* it was shed. A coat of arms won in a
crusade is worth a thousand slavering compliments bandied
about amongst a rabble.

If Lovecraft was a gentleman, he was also a pessimist. Influenced
by Schopenhauer's pessimism and Nietzsche's genealogy of morals, he
believed that the average person was just that — average, meaning
pleasure-seeking, lazy, and mediocre. For a nation or a culture to grow
in vital power, he believed that a strong leader must be at its head to
curb the rabble and focus its destructive energies. That is why Lovecraft was an early supporter of Mussolini and Hitler. Lovecraft's read-
ership will lie with an elite citizenship possessing a learned vocabulary.
It is they who may adapt Lovecraft's world view and style of weird
entertainment to the cauldron of popular culture and possibly shock a
new generation with the dangers of Dunwich, Innsmouth, and Red
Hook.

Selected Bibliography

Works by Lovecraft

Lovecraft, H.P. *The Annotated H.P. Lovecraft*. Annotated and edited with an introduction by S.T. Joshi. New York: Dell, 1997.

_____. *At the Mountains of Madness* (corrected sixth printing). Sauk City, Wisconsin: Arkham House, 1965.

_____. *Dagon and Other Macabre Tales* (corrected sixth printing). Sauk City, Wisconsin: Arkham House, 1965.

_____. *The Dunwich Horror* (corrected sixth printing). Sauk City, Wisconsin: Arkham House, 1965.

_____. *Fungi from Yuggoth and Other Poems* (formerly titled *Collected Poems*). New York: Ballantine Books, 1963.

_____. *The Horror in the Museum* (corrected sixth printing). Sauk City, Wisconsin: Arkham House, 1965.

_____. *Lord of a Visible World: An Autobiography in Letters* (edited by S. T. Joshi and David E. Schultz). Athens: Ohio University Press, 2000.

_____. *More Annotated H. P. Lovecraft* (annotated by S. T. Joshi and Peter Cannon). New York: Dell, 1999.

"Collaborations" by Lovecraft and Derleth

Lovecraft, H.P., and August Derleth. *The Lurker at the Threshold*. New York: Beagle Books, 1945.

_____. *The Shuttered Room and Other Pieces*. Sauk City, Wisconsin: Arkham House, 1957.

_____. *The Survivor and Others*. New York: Ballantine Books, 1957.

Books and Articles About Lovecraft

Daniel, Dennis. "Lovecraft Lives." *Deep Red*, no. 3 (June 1988).

De Camp, L. Sprague. *Lovecraft: A Biography*. Garden City, New York: Doubleday, 1975.

Derleth, August. *Some Notes on H.P. Lovecraft*. Sauk City, Wisconsin: Arkham House, 1959.

Joshi, S.T. *H P. Lovecraft: A Life*. Necronomicon Press, 1996.

Critical Writings on Lovecraft

Carter, Lin. *Lovecraft: A Look Behind the Cthulhu Mythos*. New York: Ballantine, 1972.

Joshi, S.T. *H.P. Lovecraft: The Decline of the West*. Berkeley Heights, New Jersey: Wildside Press, 1990.

_____. *A Subtler Magick: The Writings and Philosophy of H.P. Lovecraft*. Gilette, New Jersey: Wildside Press, 1999.

_____, ed. *H.P. Lovecraft: Four Decades of Criticism*. Athens: Ohio University Press, 1980.

Levy, Maurice. *Lovecraft: A Study in the Fantastic*. Detroit: Wayne State University Press, 1988.

Schweitzer, Darrell. *The Dream Quest of H.P. Lovecraft*. San Bernadino: Borgo Press, 1978.

Shreffler, Philip A. *The H.P. Lovecraft Companion*. Westport, Connecticut: Greenwood Press, 1977.

Critical Works on Lovecraft in Popular Culture

Migliore, Andrew, and John Strysik. *The Lurker in the Lobby: A Guide to the Cinema of H. P. Lovecraft*. Seattle: Armitage House, 2000.

"M.M. Interviews Nick Adams." *Modern Monsters*, no. 1 (June 1966).

Norton, Haywood P. "The Strange Case of H.P. Lovecraft." *Castle of Frankenstein*, no. 18 (1972).

Nutman, Philip. "Re-Animator: An Interview with Brian Yuzna." *Starburst*, vol. 8, no. 7 (March 1986).

Parry, Michael. "A Visit to the Set of *Die Monster Die*." *Castle of Frankenstein*, no. 7 (1965).

Rebello, Stephen. "Stuart Gordon — The Genre's Re-Animator." *Cinefantastique*, vol. 17, no. 1 (1987).

Lovecraft Fanzines

Fanzines are often more informative than prozines. An example is *Nyctalops*, edited and published by Harry O. Morris, Jr., out of Albuquerque, New Mexico, in the early seventies. Most of what appears here is both scholarly and engaging.

Index